SAPCOOKBOOK Training Tutorials for MM Purchasing

Michael M. Martinez

EQUITY PRESS

SAP MM Training Tutorials: SAP MM Purchasing Essentials Guide: SAPCOOKBOOK Training Tutorials for MM Purchasing

ISBN 978-1-60332-130-3

Edited by Jamie Sever

The programs in this book have been included for instructional value only. They have been tested with care but are not guaranteed for any particular purpose. The publisher does not offer any warranties or representations and does not accept any liabilities with respect to the programs.

Printed in the United States of America

Please visit our website at www.sapcookbook.com

TABLE OF CONTENTS

Introduction to SAPCOOKBOOK Training Tutorials

As the cover of this book states, "SAPCOOKBOOK Training Tutorials are the fastest way to Learn SAP, period." I really believe this is true. The cover continues...

"SAPCOOKBOOK Training Tutorials are designed to help you understand what you need to know to get started working in SAP. Written from the end-user's perspective, SAPCOOKBOOK Training Tutorials provide step-by-step instruction on how to execute the critical transactions in each functional area of SAP. This is not a 1000-page reference manual filled with obscure configuration items that you will never use — this book shows you what people actually do in the SAP system."

Now when you start interviewing and working in SAP, you're going to encounter a peculiar attitude. That is: Welcome to SAP. Now go home! That's the attitude I've come to expect from established SAP professionals, and from SAP itself. Especially when you're like me and don't believe in keeping secrets or overcharging your clients — you'll encounter this attitude at every turn.

So be warned that this book isn't for everyone, and it might even be a little bit dangerous. I say this mostly because I encourage a self-training philosophy that is counter to what many established consultants and SAP professionals believe. And you may have to hide this philosophy from others in the business who are generally a conservative bunch.

Many of the people who won't approve of this book believe that if you want to break into SAP that you should somehow go through what they had to go through in order to get a job. Meaning that they want you to spend a pile of money, and they want you to suffer as they did — grinding away for years learning and studying. Or they want you to get into SAP by luck, which is how they got into the business, and of course we can't rely on luck as a plan for our lives. Of course, if you have lots of money and lots of time — by all means, please devote it all to the study of SAP.

But most of all, I believe that established professionals in SAP will not like this book because they want to keep you out of SAP. They don't want any more competition, and so I fully expect this book to draw criticism and negative reviews from people who think I'm trying to give away their secrets. Well, I don't believe in secrets – not in the age of information.

I think that this old way of thinking about a career in SAP just isn't realistic. Because formal training in SAP is expensive, time consuming, there are no secrets anymore, and my core philosophy is that spending time and money to learn skills before you put them into use is risky.

Another component of my philosophy is that I believe that large companies have broken the contract of employment – individuals can no longer rely on businesses to "take care of them" with pensions, perhaps as our forefathers could. Now companies want you to arrive pre-trained (pushing the training cost to you) with skills that they need (pushing the risk of learning these skills to you) and when they don't need the skill any more, they push you out of the door (saving themselves money).

So since big corporations have broken the contract of employment, I really think it's appropriate for you, the humble worker or employee, to break a contract or two yourself. You don't need to fall in line and do things the old way "just because."

The "flat world" of work and life doesn't just *favor* people who can make themselves temporarily useful to big companies – it *demands* that they can quickly acquire useful skills to meet market demand, and then when the demand for these skills wanes, they must be ready to learn another useful skill set – and put this to work immediately.

So I'm going to make some statements that are guaranteed to upset SAP professionals who have been working in the business their entire careers, who think SAP knowledge is somehow privileged information to be kept to themselves.

So welcome to *Breaking Into SAP*. This book is the culmination of my career in Information Technology, and it's a distillation of my unique experiences in the marketplace, working in the SAP business for about 14 years.

This is a book about how to break into SAP, but then again, I also think the material applies to your entire career in Information Technology and business.

I'm really excited about this book, and the online training program I've developed as a companion to this book. I hope you get as much out of this book as I enjoyed making it — my feeling is that there are far too many formal books out there that distance the reader with difficult language. Books that try to show you all of the configuration or technical matter that is associated with the

SAP software. I don't want this book to be like all those books that end up unread, unutilized, and in the trash bin. Please think of this book as an open conversation between you and me.

I'd like you to think of this book as a philosophy that you can use to guide your learning and your future work.

In this book, I will cover everything you will need to know to be a success in SAP, from how to prepare your resume to how to talk to recruiters. I'll discuss all the things that are necessary to get your foot into the door in SAP, and then I'll show you how to move from a permanent employee to a consultant and then to a contractor — if you so desire.

If you doubt my methods, that's fine — but please acknowledge and understand that I'm professing this path because it is the path I have taken personally. Yes, I have done this myself, and I continue to employ these methods. I do not posses any formal certification or training in SAP, yet I have risen to the highest levels of work (and compensation) in the SAP business. And this is my understanding of the business, and how you can get there. And again, my mantra is "Always be breaking into SAP." You're going to take the steps in this book and apply them over and over in your career.

So again, welcome, and I do hope you enjoy the material we've provided here. We do offer a more comprehensive self-study course that normally accompany this manual — the training includes training video, online system access to a practice SAP system, and you can get this training at www.sapcookbook.com.

OK! With that introduction, let's jump right into it and get to the essentials.

The SAP GUI, Graphical User Interface

Before we begin our discussion of Purchase Requisitions and Purchase Orders, we will have a quick review of the SAP GUI. You will need to have downloaded and installed the SAP Logon software. **This tutorial will use SAP Logon 640 software, but you can also use SAP Logon 710 release software.** We will log into an **"SAP Client".** SAP is a client-based system where you need to enter a three-digit number that defines the client. The client is the highest level in SAP.

To begin with, select the logon shortcut SAP Logon 640 icon to start the logon software.

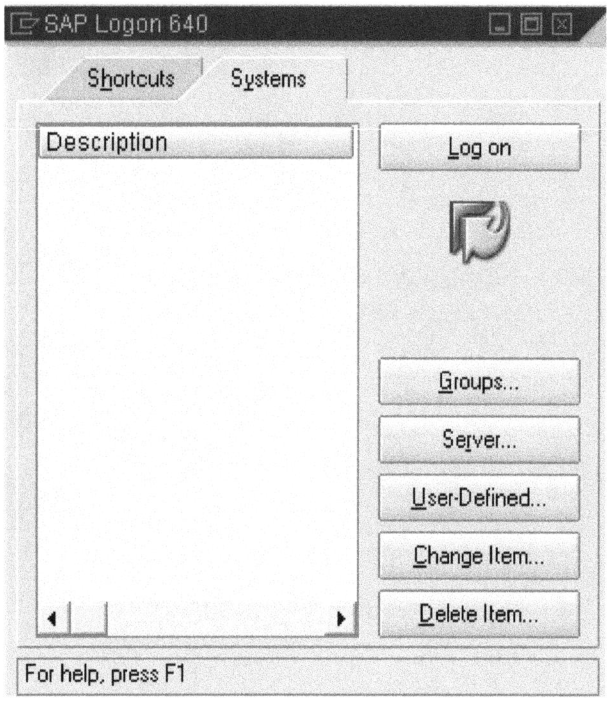

If you just installed the logon software or you don't have the SAP Cookbook server set up yet, you will need to enter the servers System Connection Parameters. Select the User-Defined button [User-Defined...] on the Logon screen. If you are using 710, select the new item button [New Item...] on the Logon screen.

For SAP Logon 710 users, the Create New System Entry screen comes up. Highlight the User Specified System item and select **NEXT.** This is not a concern for 640 users.

On the System tab or for 710 users, the Connection tab, we enter a Description, Application Server, System Number and the System ID received from SAP Cookbook. Also ensure to toggle the R/3 radio button.

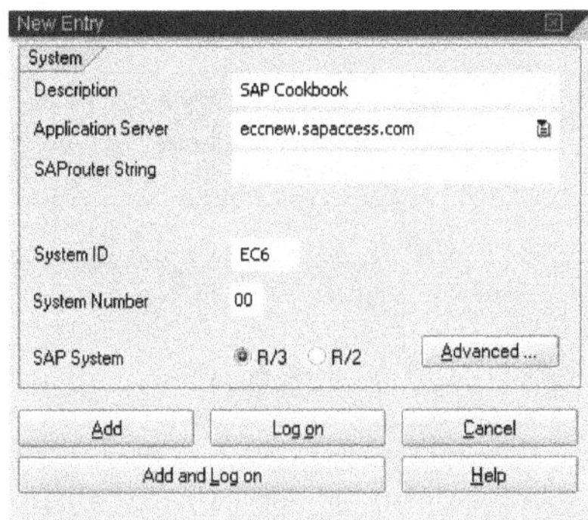

Access to Live ECC 6.0 IDES Server

Description:	SAP ECC
Application Server:	eccnew.sapaccess.com
SAP routing string:	<leave blank>
System ID:	EC6
System Number:	00
Client:	100

After entering data, select **Add** and your logon software will be ready to access SAP Cookbooks training server. For 710 users, select OK followed by Finish.

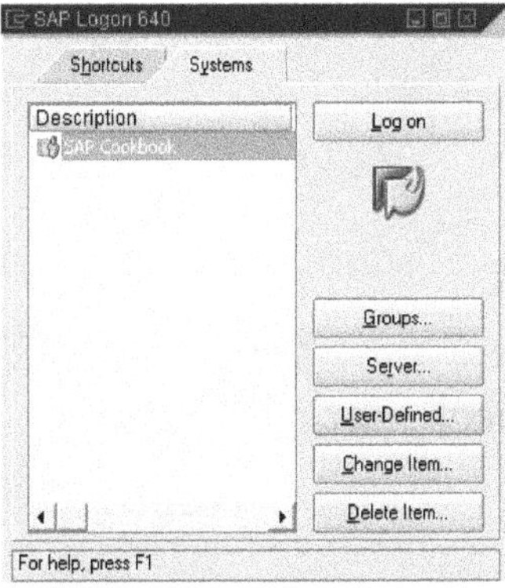

The SAP Logon software is now set up and the SAP Cookbook training server is now available to be logged onto.

Select the LOGON button and the SAP Cookbooks ECC 6.0 training client Log On screen comes up. An SAP system can have multiple clients, such as a Training Client, a Production Client, and Development Client etc. Each has its own specific 3-digit identifier. We will work on the ECC 6.0 Client 100.

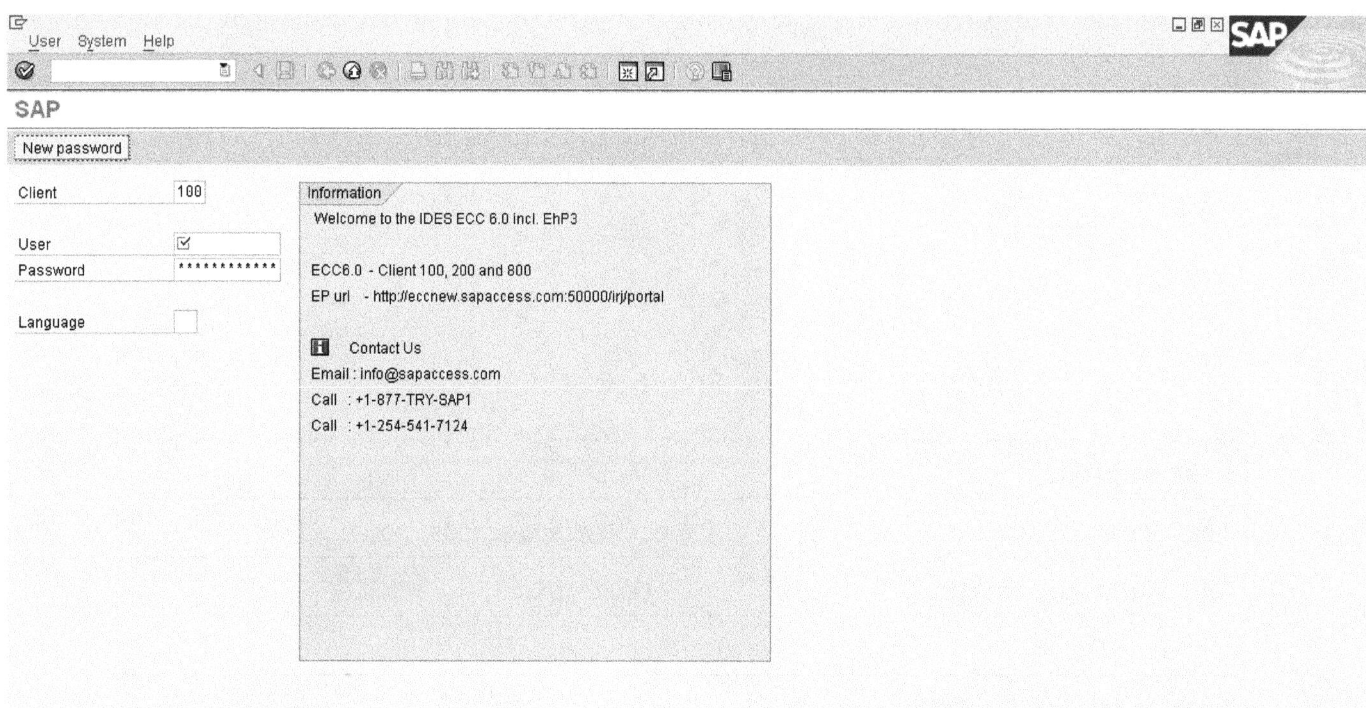

Notice the **User** field has a ***box with a check mark*** in it. Any time in SAP you see a field with a box and a check mark, it is a MANDATORY FIELD. **SAP will not complete transactions with incomplete mandatory fields.**

SAP Cookbook will have issued you a User Name and have set up your password.

Your User Name is: ________________________________

Your Password is: ________________________________

After entering the client, your user ID and your password, select the green check mark or hit enter.

The **SAP Easy Access** screen comes up. From this screen, we can begin all transactions within SAP that we are authorized to perform.

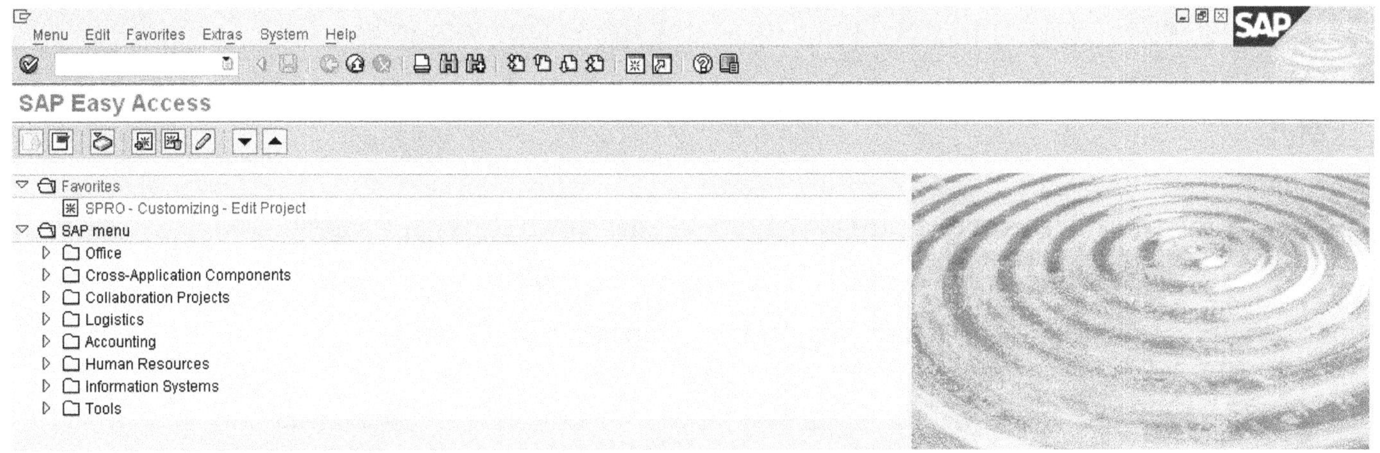

The **SAP Menu Bar** is located across the top of the screen.

This bar changes depending upon the screen you are in, but the **System** and **Help** options are always present. The menu bar provides access to certain transactions and functions.

Below the SAP menu bar is the **SAP Standard Toolbar**.

Notice the **Green Check Mark** icon. Pressing this is the same as pressing **Enter** on your keyboard.

The white field located next to the green check mark icon is the **Command Field**. Here is where you can enter known **Transaction Codes** which are shortcuts to various screens in SAP. There are THOUSANDS (16000+) of transaction codes in SAP. By entering known transaction codes here, you do not need to navigate the SAP menu tree to find a specific transaction. The Command Field can be hidden by clicking on the triangle next to the field.

The **SAVE icon** is used to save your work or post transactions in SAP.

The **Green Arrow** icon is used to go BACK one screen, the **Yellow Arrow** is EXIT and the **Red X** is Cancel.

The **Printer icon** is for printing and the **Binocular icons** are for searching.

The **four Page icons** with arrows are for paging up and down through a screen. You use these to page one screen at a time or all the way to the top or bottom. Some screens can get very lengthy and the use of the search and page features can come in handy.

The **Create Another Session** icon is helpful when running multiple transactions.

The **Shortcut Link** icon creates a shortcut to the session your in on your desktop. This is helpful if you run the same transaction many times throughout the day.

The **Round Question Mark** icon is a help button. If you have a question about something in SAP, place your cursor on the field in question and select this icon. Information about that particular field will come up in a pop-up window.

The **Settings** button icon allows you to make changes to various screens setting.

Below the SAP standard toolbar is the title bar. It describes the screen your in. Currently you are in the **SAP Easy Access** screen.

SAP Easy Access

The **Application Bar** is next. **This row of icons changes throughout SAP as you navigate from transaction to transaction.**

The SAP menu icon is handy in that it collapses the menu tree completely. As you navigate the tree, many directories will open up and the tree can become cumbersome to maneuver through. Click on the SAP icon and the tree collapses completely.

The **Status Bar** is located at the bottom left of the screen. All SAP messages, errors and warnings appear here. The **Information Field** is located on the bottom right of the screen. Information on the system and TRANSACTION CODES appear here. The Information Field can be hidden by clicking on the triangle next to the field.

The List Detail icon, , is seen throughout SAP. This icon will display a list of possible selections that are available on a particular window or screen. Click on the icon, select the item Transaction and now the transaction code that you last selected will show up in the Information Field.

IMPORTANT: Ensure that the technical names can be seen in the directories. On the menu bar select **Extras > Settings** and toggle the ***Display technical names*** box, and then Enter. This ensures that we can see the **TRANSACTION CODES**.

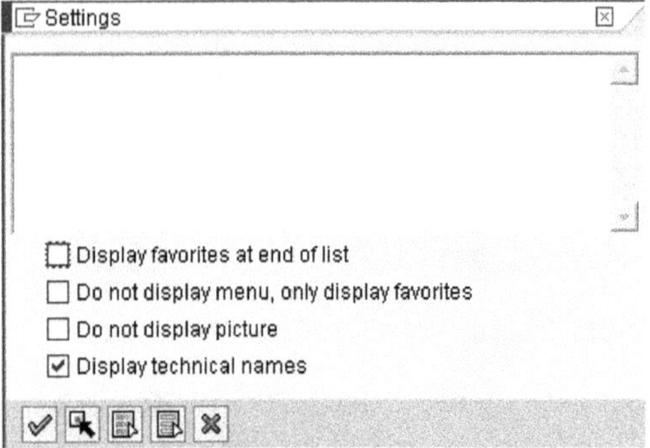

To Log Off the SAP system, on the menu bar select **System > Log Off.** A warning to save your work comes up before you log off.

The Purchase Requisition

The Purchase Requisition is the first step in creating a demand for a material or service. It is the procedure by which SAP users or departments can request the purchase of goods or services that require processing by your purchasing department. Like many aspects of SAP, you will need authorization to create a purchase requisition. See your supervisor or SAP security department on receiving the proper authorizations.

The Purchase Requisition can either be entered manually by an SAP user or it can be automatically generated via a Material Requirements Planning (MRP) system. This includes Purchase Requisitions created by Production Orders, by Plant Maintenance Orders, by Project Systems or by Materials Planning. The majority of **non-production** purchase requisitions are created directly by an SAP user and not by other SAP functionalities. The most common way to create a requisition is by using an item or service **Material Master**. The Purchase Requisition for materials that have a Material Master Record requires, at a minimum, the following to be entered.

1) A Material Number for the Item or Service being requested

2) A quantity for the item requested will need to be entered

3) The Units of Measure for the item will need to be entered

4) The delivery date desired will also need to be entered

SAP will issue warnings if required information is missing. Creating your own **Personal Settings** will help with this. Before creating a Purchase Requisition it is often useful to review the Material Master of the item or service desired. There is useful information that organizations enter into a material master that will need to be entered into the Purchase Requisitions. Many organizations enter the Purchasing Group responsible for a particular item or service on the Basic Data 2 screen, or Purchasing Screen in a Material Master, which will need to be transferred to the Purchase Requisition. Also, if you know what vendor to use, there may be information in the **Vendor Master** that you may want for the Purchase Requisition. Let's review both record types and then create a Purchase Requisition.

MM03 Displaying Material Master Data

Objective: To display a Material Master record to search for additional data for use on a Purchase Requisition.

SAP Menu Path:

> **Logistics > Materials Management > Material Master > Material > Display> MM03 Display current**

The **DISPLAY MATERIAL (Initial Screen)** comes up.

Enter a Material Number that you're interested in. In this example, we are interested in quarts of 10W30 Motor Oil, Material Number 1500-500. Input the number in the Material field and select Enter or the Green check mark. When you enter a material number for a material master, SAP wants to know what screens of the material master you wish to view. These selections are made on the Select View(s) screen.

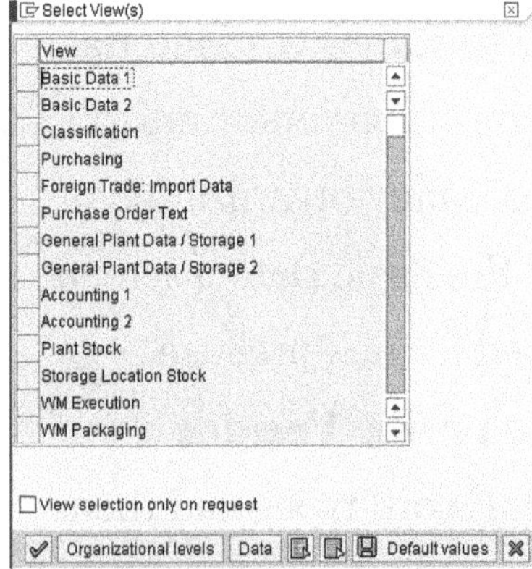

Here we will select Basic Data 1, Basic Data 2, Purchasing, Purchase Order Text and Accounting 1. After making your view selections, select the green check mark.

Before displaying the material master, SAP wants to know if you want to use any particular plant or valuation type. This helps narrow down the amount of data you will view. You can simply leave it blank and select the green check mark or enter a plant in case there is plant specific information we may possibly want to see. **In this example we will use the search facility, [icon], next to plant to find and choose plant 3000 New York.**

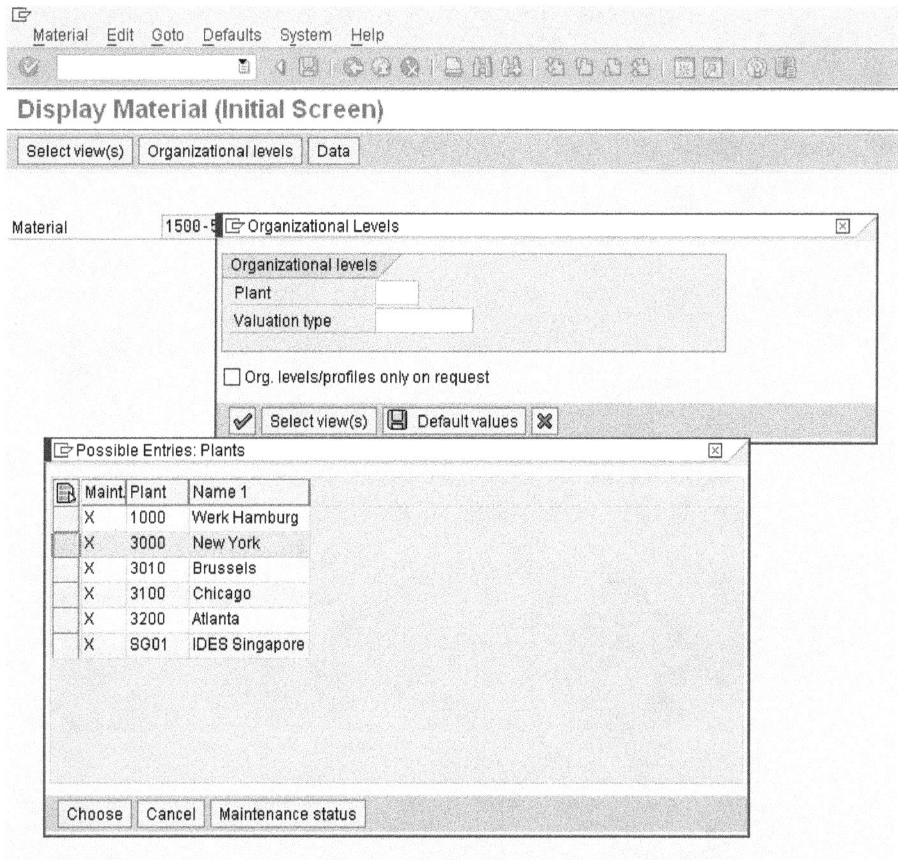

The **Display Material 1500-500 (Operating Supplies)** screen comes up. On this screen, you can view each individual tab by selecting the particular tab of interest or use the List Detail drop down icon on the top right to select the tab directly from a list. Notice that the tabs you highlighted previously are now marked.

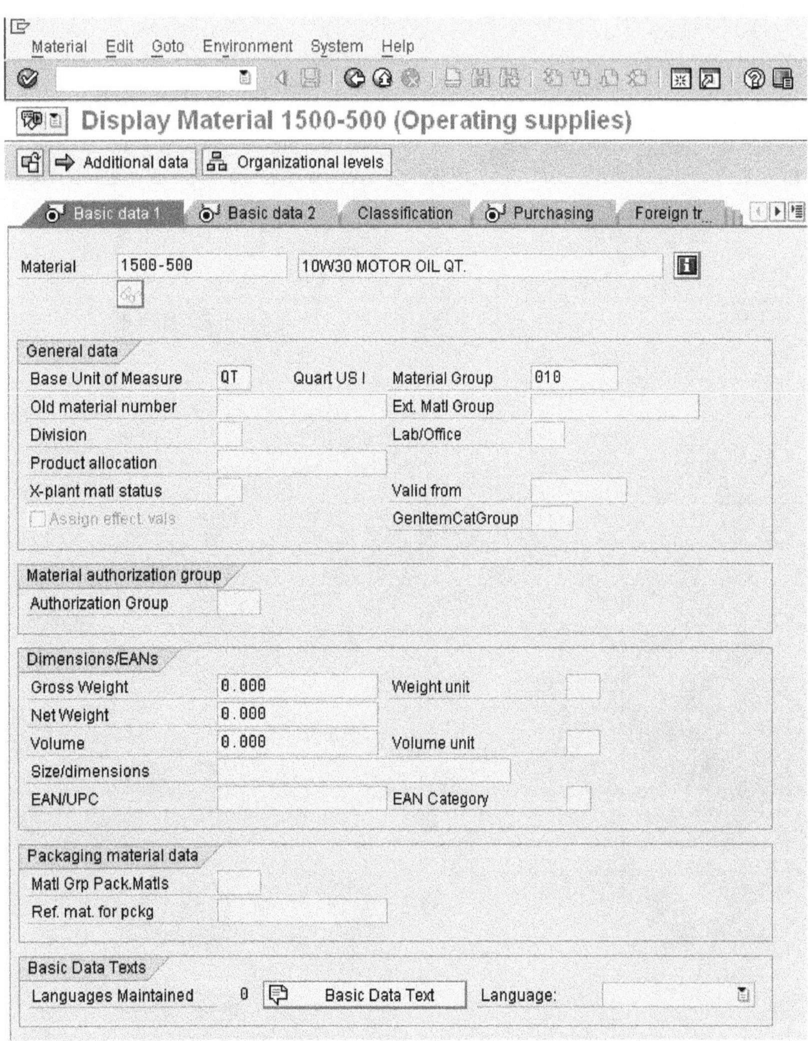

The first page/tab of the **Material Master** is the ***Basic Data 1 screen.*** Here we see the material number and a description of the material. The base units of measure are defined here and are how they should be used in the Purchase Requisition as well as a material group and any information that may help in describing the item or service. You may also find "Legacy Data and Information" about the material such as an Old material number. By selecting the **Additional Data** button leads to a detailed description screen of the material.

The second page/tab of the **Material Master** is the ***Basic Data 2 screen.*** Here there is often information on Purchasing Groups and other general text information about the item or service. This is a great place to locate more information to make the purchasing of an item easier for the user creating the requisition as well as the buyer. Data on this page can be manually entered into the purchase requisition if it is available.

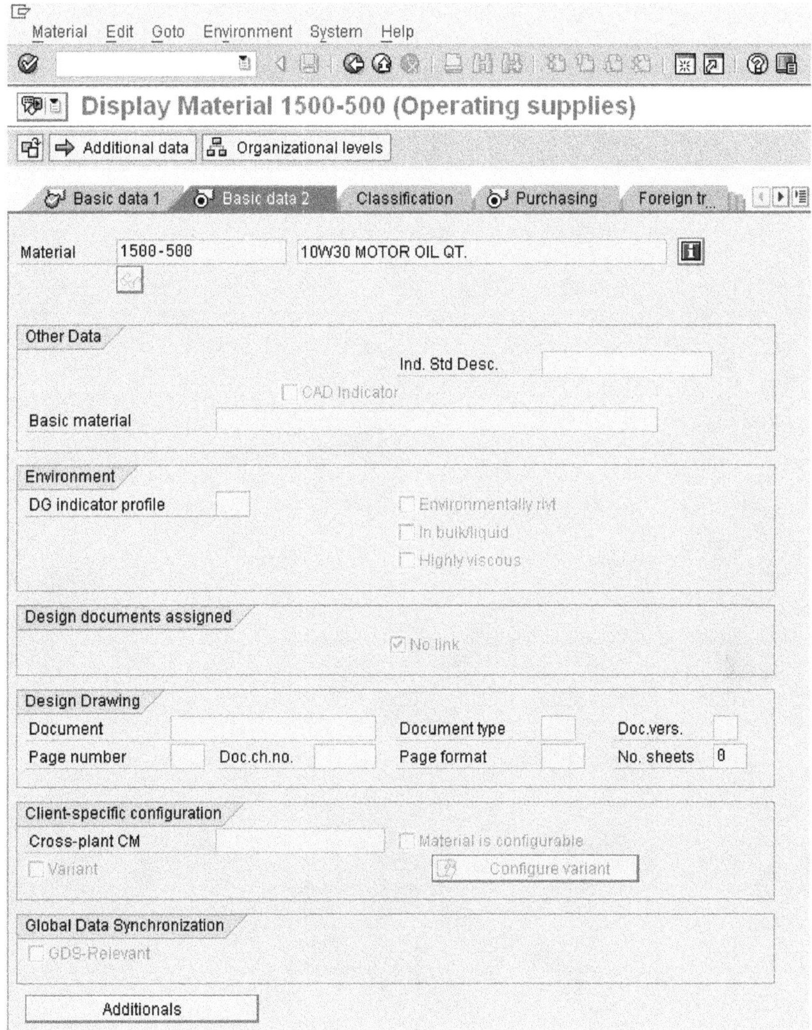

Notice that after you have reviewed a tab that was initially selected, a green check mark appears to remind you that you have viewed that particular tab already.

The next tab that we are interested in is the **Purchasing** tab. This is where you will find the **Purchasing Group** number and the **Material Group** number used in creating purchase requisitions. **Your Purchasing Department may request that you supply the Purchasing Group responsible for the item or service you are requesting, along with the Material Group in the Purchase Requisition.**

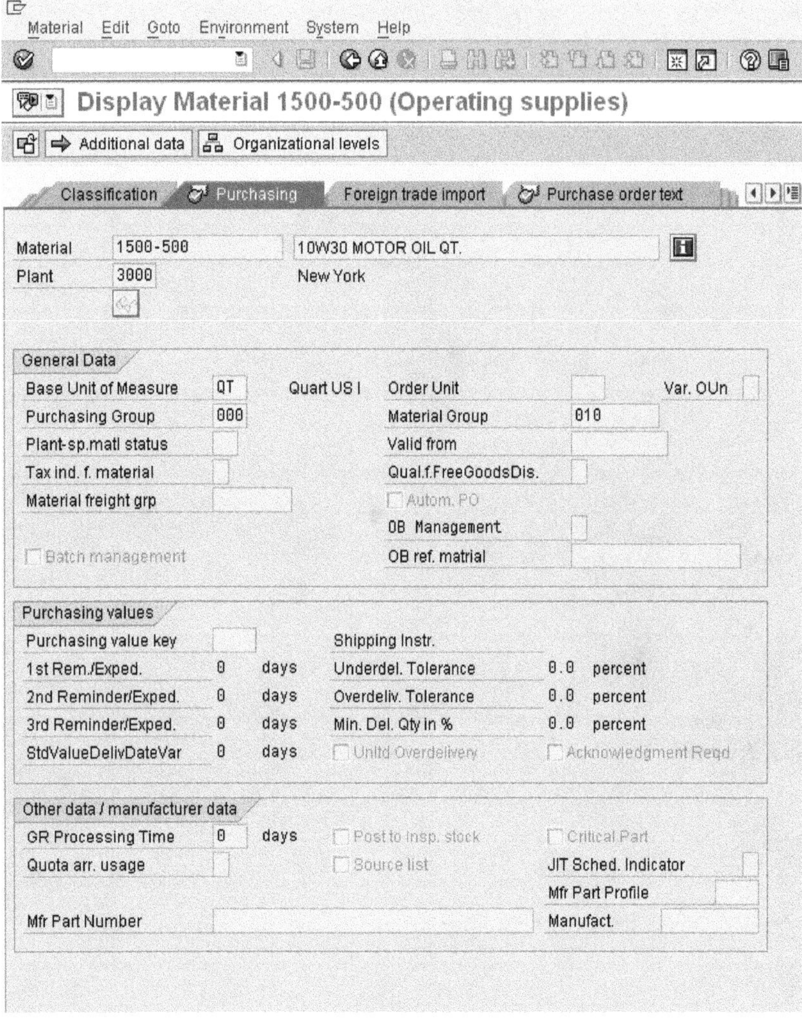

The next tab we are going to look at is the Purchase Order Text. This text will often default into a purchase order to save on typing and eliminate errors on materials that are ordered often.

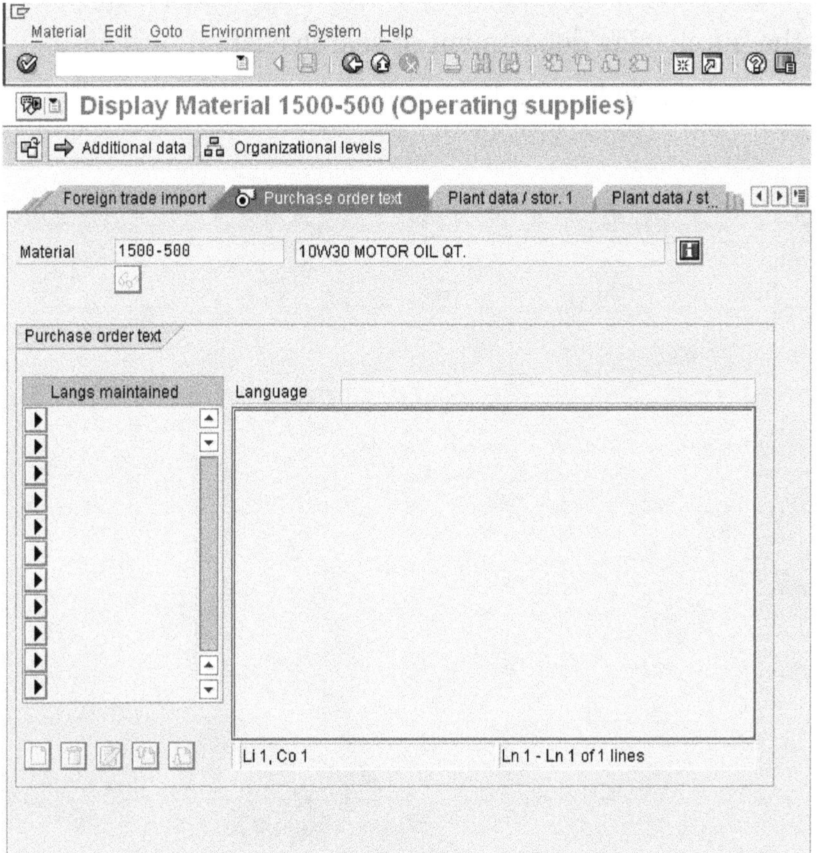

The final tab we will look at in this exercise is the Accounting 1 tab. Here we see the Base Unit of Measure and currency used to purchase the material. Of importance is the Valuation Price. **This price IS NEEDED in order to complete the Purchase Requisition.** If the price isn't available on the Material Master, contact the purchasing department or search current purchase requisitions and purchase orders for the most recent Valuation Price used.

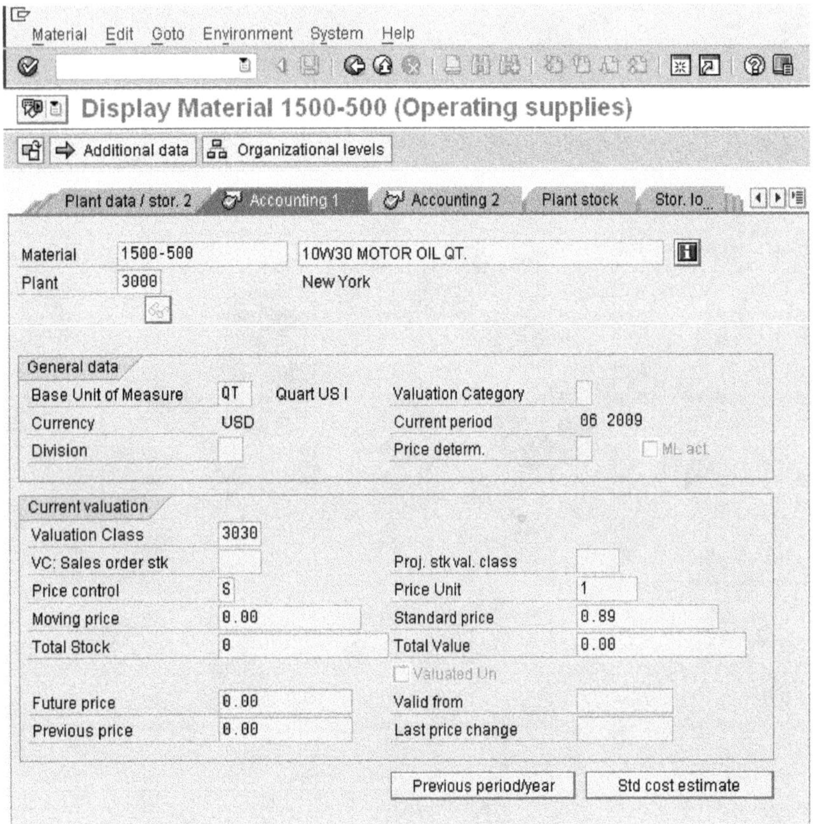

MK03 Displaying Vendor Master Data

Objective: To display the Vendor Master Data for a company.

SAP Menu Path:

> **Logistics > Materials Management > Purchasing > Master Data > Vendor > Purchasing > MK03 - Display (current)**

The **Display Vendor (Master): Initial Screen** is now displayed:

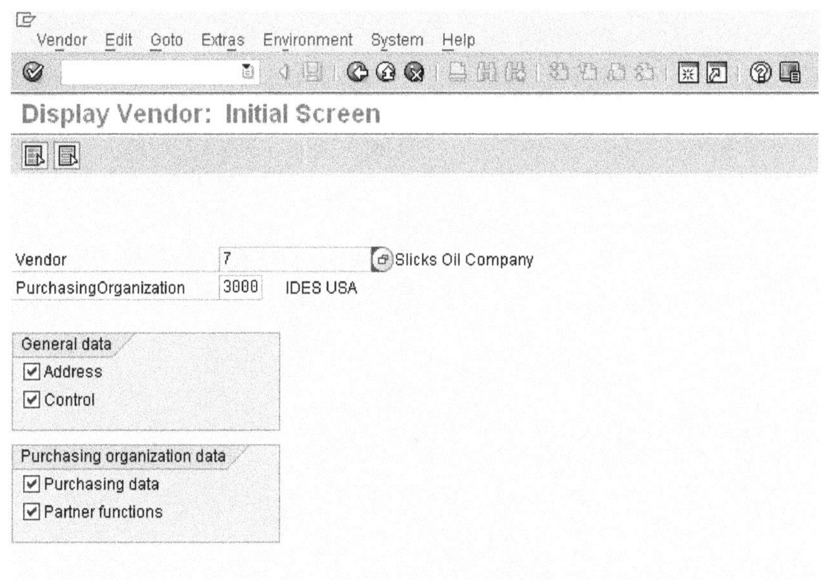

Enter Vendor # 7 and Purchasing Organization 3000

Click on the select all button to view all vendor data and then select the green check mark.

The first page of the **Vendor Master** is the ***Address Page.*** The vendor's name, address, language, phone number and email address are usually located here. Other forms of communication can also be set up such as fax machine numbers and mobile phones.

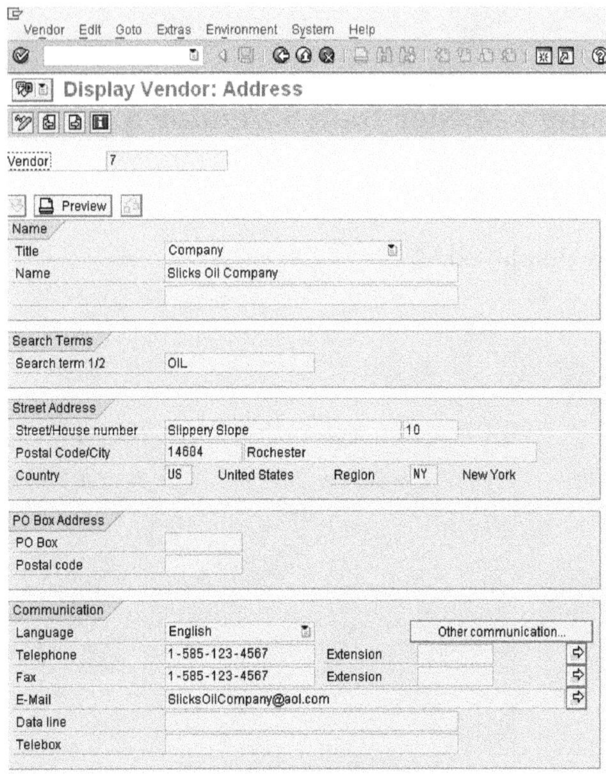

Select the next page icon .

The second page (**select next page icon**) of the **Vendor Master** is the ***Display Vendor: Control*** page, which contains tax information.

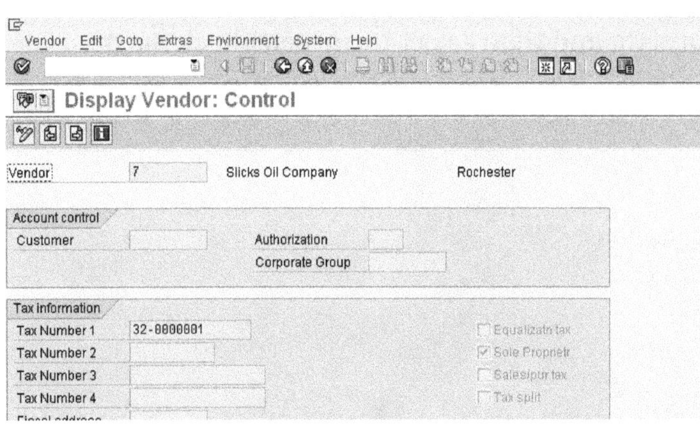

Select the next page icon .

The third page of the **Vendor Master** is the ***Display Vendor: Purchasing Data*** page. This page will usually contain a vendor contact and their phone number. Also if this is an international vendor, you will be able to see the currency used by the vendor.

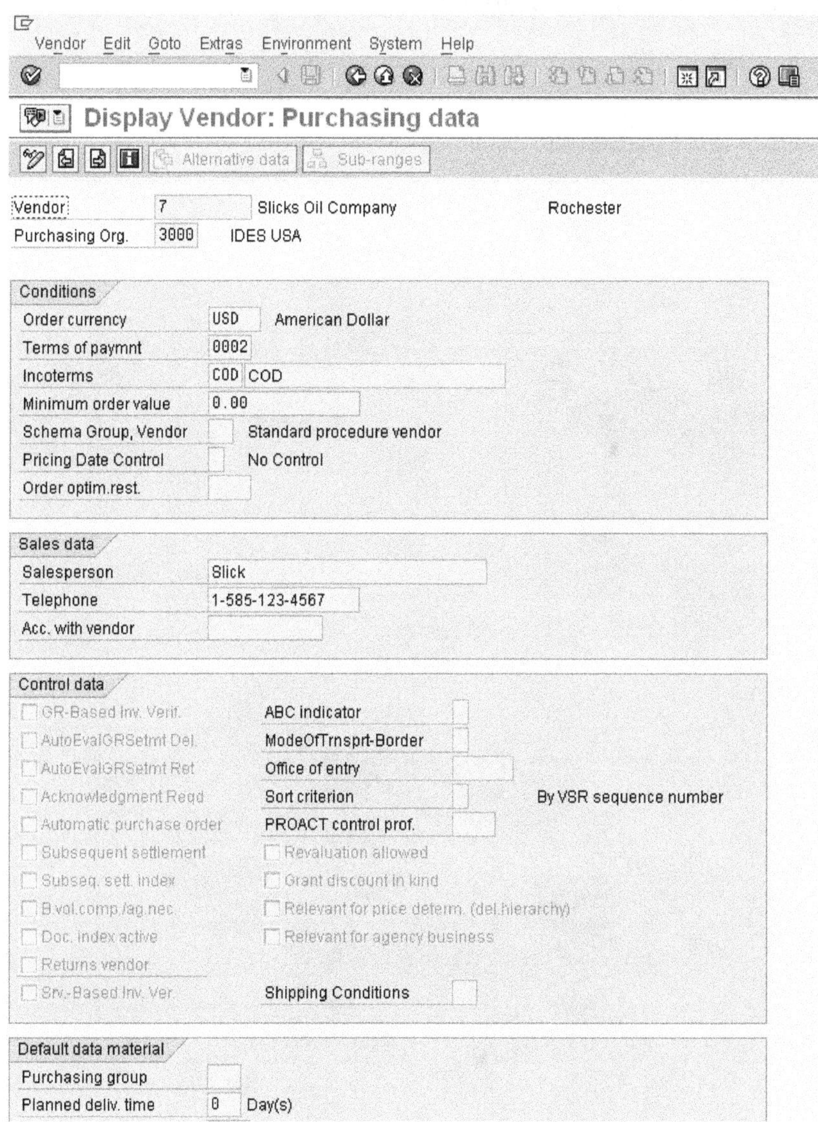

Select next page icon .

MK03 Displaying Vendor Master Data

The fourth page of the **Vendor Master** is the ***Partner Functions*** screen. This screen is used by the purchasing department to determine what function this particular vendor performs within the larger vendor organization. This is particularly useful when dealing with large vendors with multiple offices and organizational groups which are not centrally located.

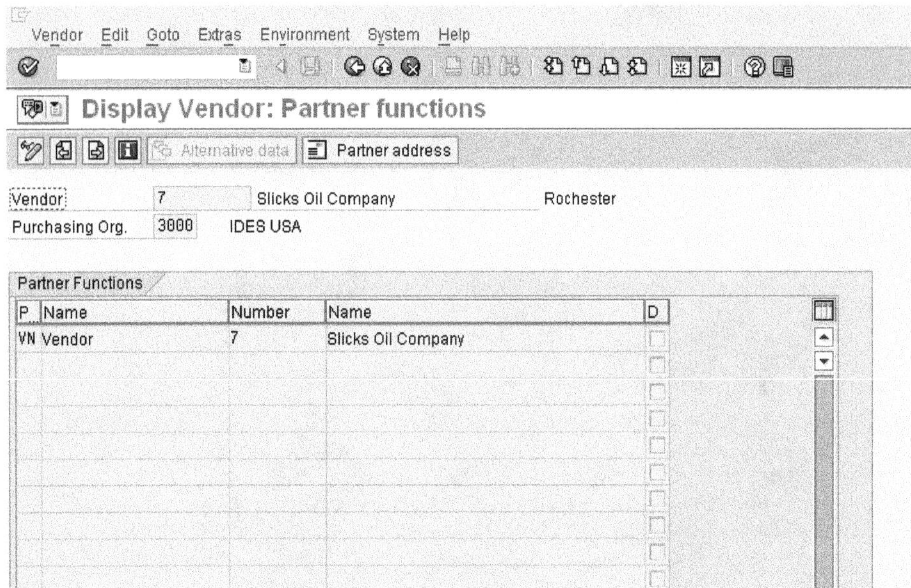

ME13 Displaying Purchasing Information Record

Objective: To display more purchasing master data information, the Info Record which contains prices.

SAP Menu Path:

> **Logistics > Materials Management > Purchasing > Master Data > Info Record > ME13 -Display**

The **DISPLAY INFO RECORD: Initial Screen** is displayed. Vendor 7, material 1500-500, Purchasing Org 3000 and Plant 3000 should default in since these are the vendor number, material number and plant we recently reviewed. If you logged off the system and back on, you will need to re-enter the data.

Select an Info Category, select standard, and then Enter or the green check mark.

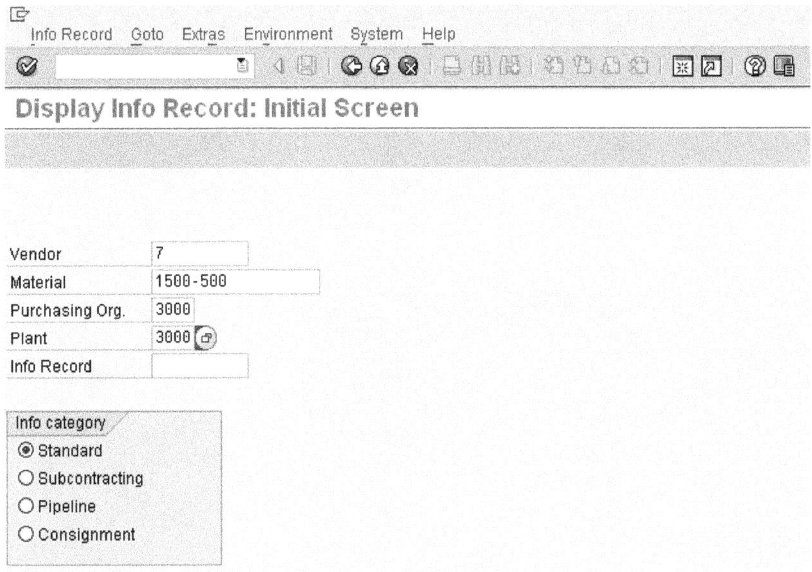

The **Display Info Record: General Data** screen comes up first and is a combination of ***specific material information from a specific vendor.*** The material number AND the material group that this material is associated with can be found. The vendor's salesperson and their telephone number can be located on this screen as well.

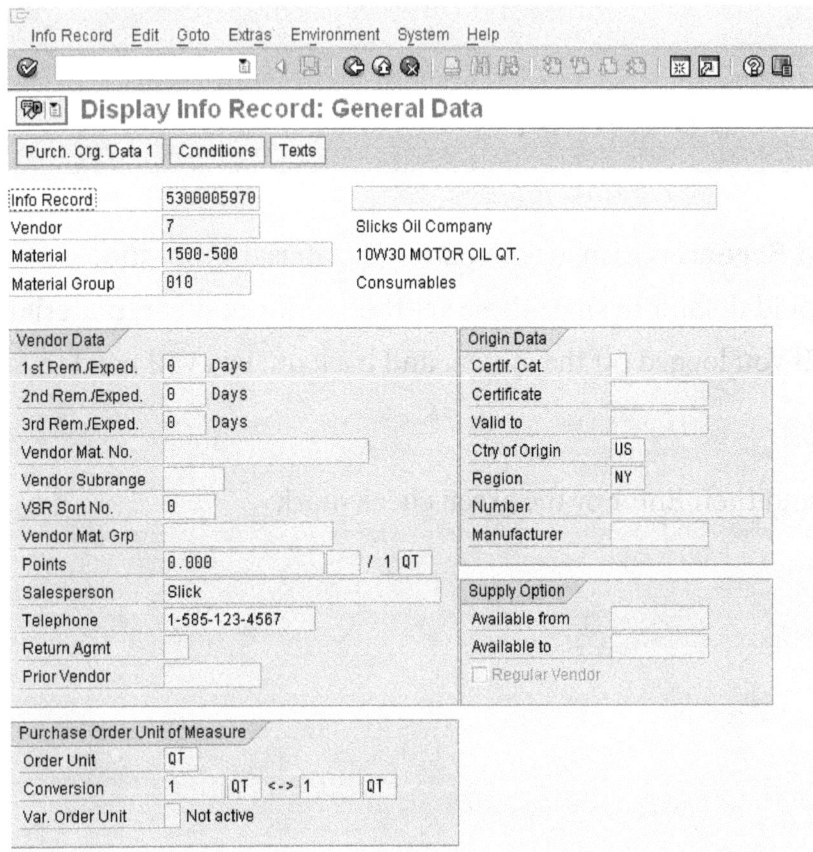

By selecting the **Purchase Organization Data 1** button, information on delivery time and net price is displayed. On the ***Control tab***, we can find information on standard order quantities and planned delivery times as well.

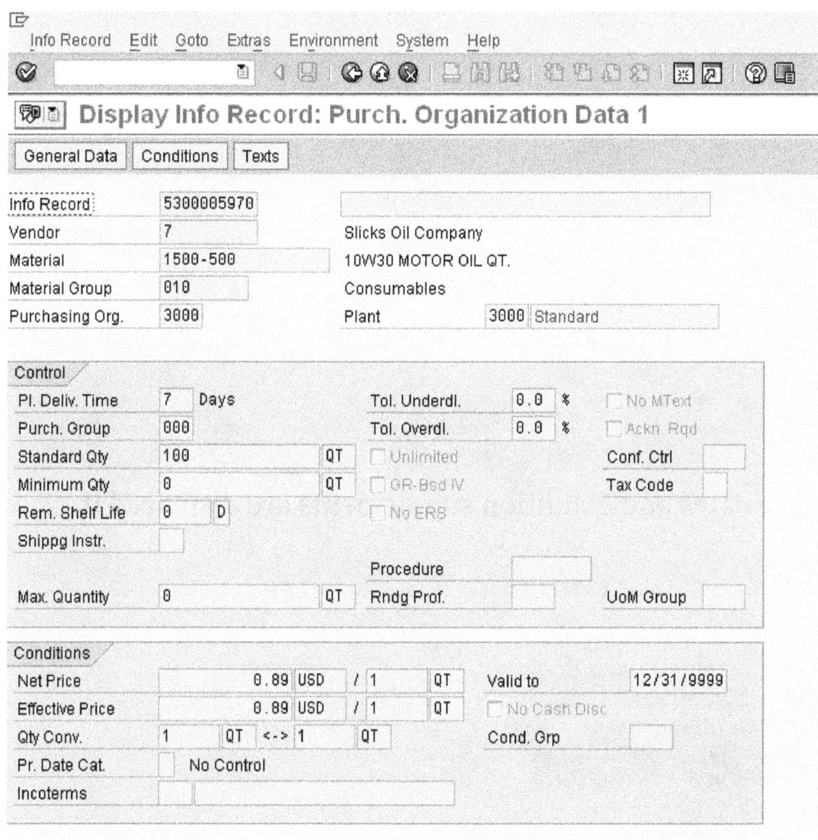

By selecting **ENTER** while on the **Purchase Organization Data 1** button, SAP goes to the **Purchase Organization Data 2** screen where information on various references is displayed.

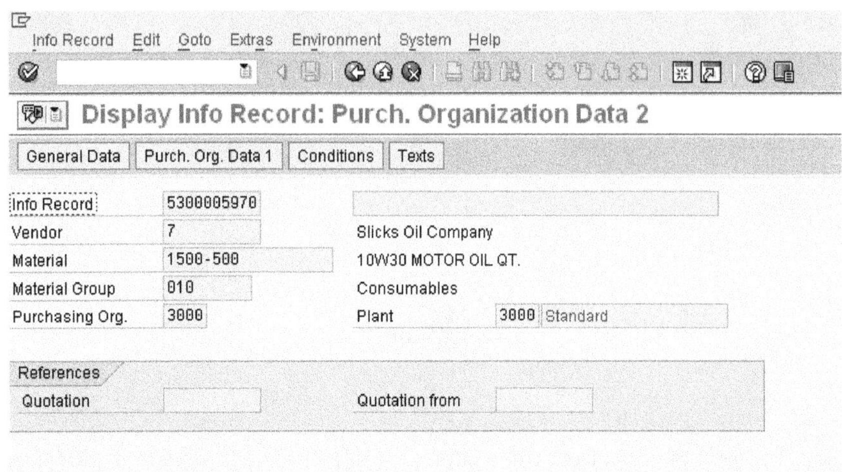

By selecting the **Conditions** button, validity dates and condition supplements are displayed if available.

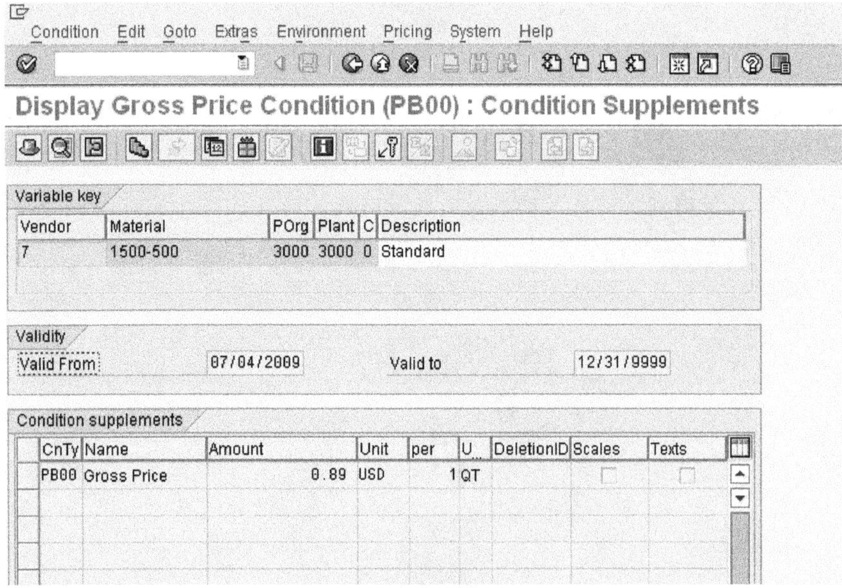

By selecting the **Texts** button, the Info Record for the material comes up. **Various texts and information that will be transferred to Purchase Orders is displayed here.** This information automatically populates the purchase order as the PO is created.

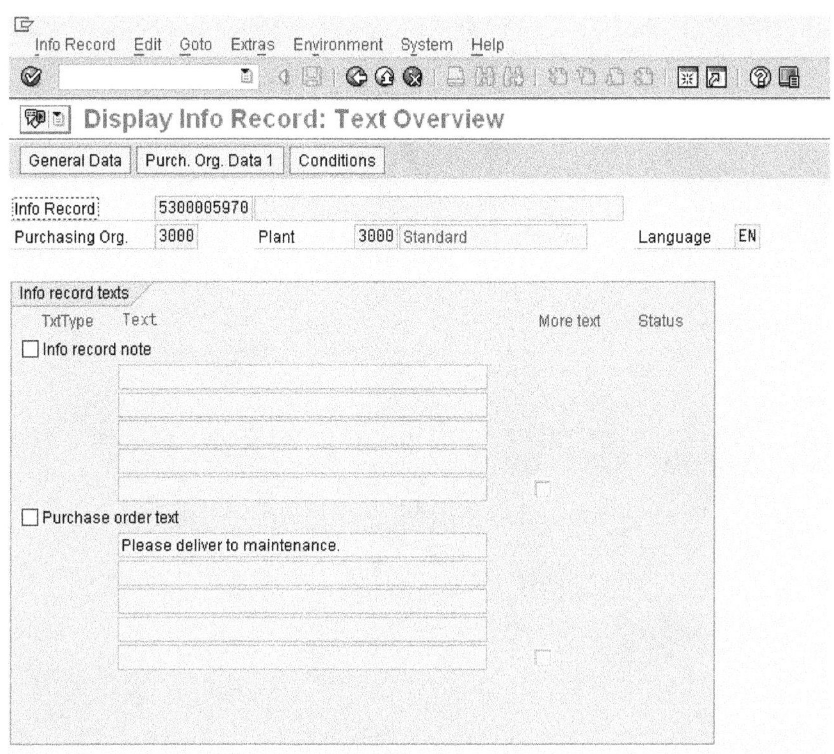

If we want to change the text that automatically goes into a PO, we need to use t-code ME12 for Changing the Purchasing Information Record. Also note that the **Info Update** check box on the PO will need to be **UNCHECKED** or the Purchase Order Text in the Info Record will be updated to reflect the latest PO entered.

ME51N Create a Purchase Requisition with a Vendor

Objective: To create a purchase requisition for a specific material. The purchase requisition is a document that *specifies the need* to create a purchase order.

SAP Menu Path:

Logistics > Materials Management > Purchasing > Purchase Requisition > ME51N - Create

The **Create Purchase Requisition** screen comes up.

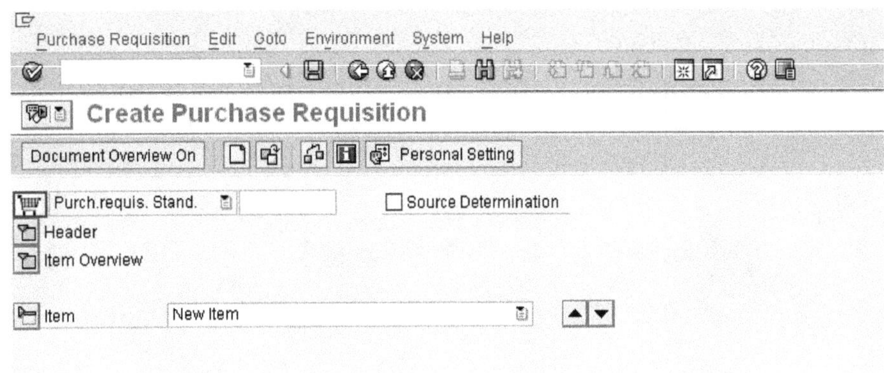

There are four sections to be filled out specific to the requisition. The first is the **Type** of requisition being created. There are several types of requisitions that can be completed. Use the list button to view the possible choices. In this example we will create a **Standard Purchase Requisition.**

Then next section is the **Header** of the requisition, Header, which contains text about the requisition. Click on the blue box to open the header. You can enter any addition details or notes about the requisition, such as a RUSH order, or on contacting you, the user.

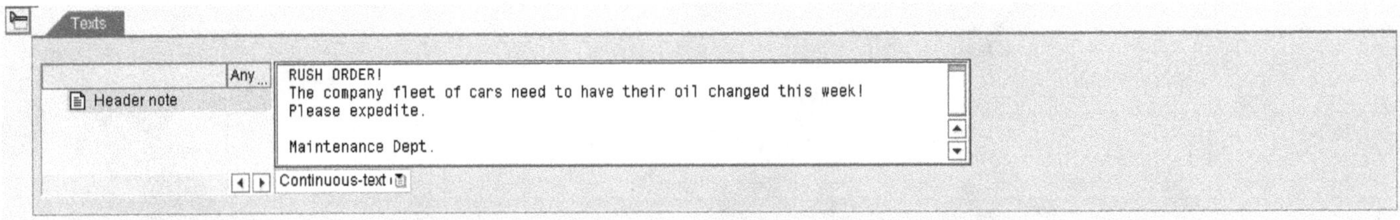

Next is the **Item Overview** section, which contains the specific information about what you are requesting. This contains the details of what is being requested.

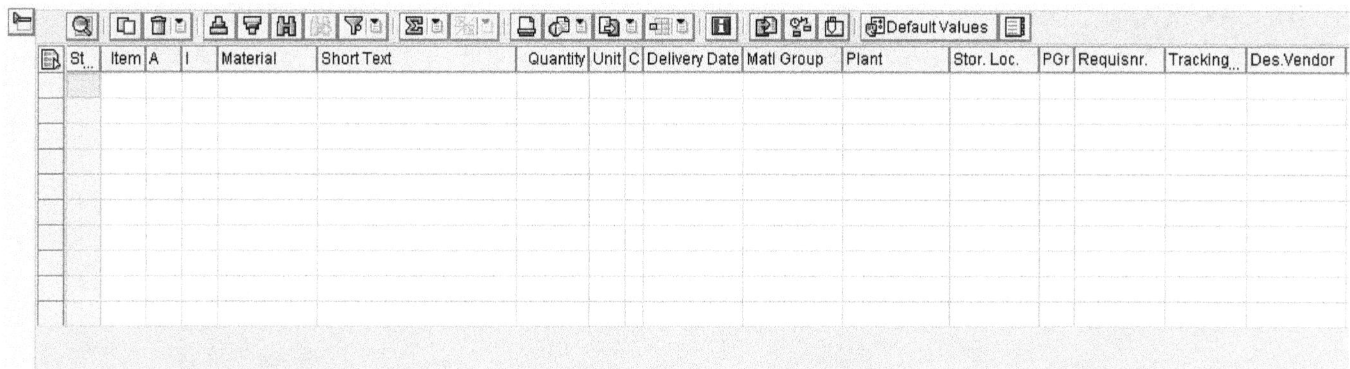

And lastly is the **Item Details** section which has addition information on materials, quantities, valuation, source of supply, status, contact person, texts delivery address and customer data. This section expands out once the Purchase Requisition is being populated.

So let's begin creating a purchase requisition for some motor oil.

```
Material: 1500-500
Quantity: 500 Quarts
Delivery Date: 12.31.09
Plant: 3000
```

NOTE: Since this is a training tutorial, the date needs to correspond to a future date. Do not use a date in the past.

First, select the **Item Overview** button which opens up a Purchase Requisition table where we can enter information about the materials being requested.

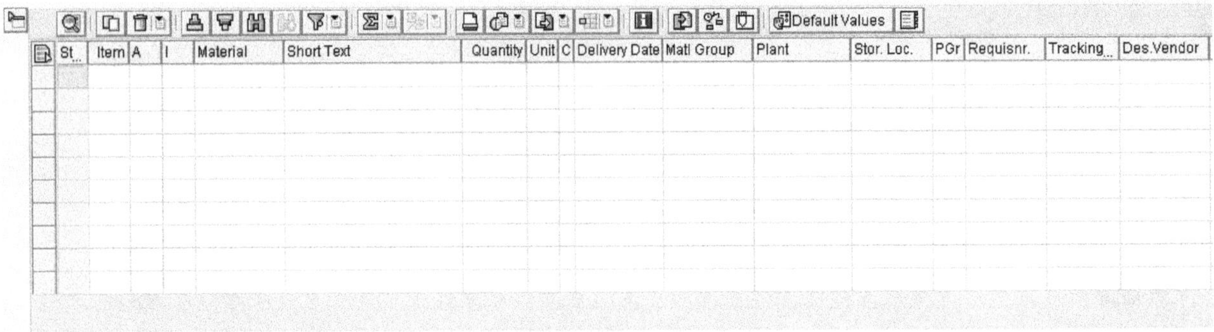

Item Numbering:

On the first row of the table, we will enter the first item requested. In the column headed Item, we begin numbering our items. It is suggested that you number items by 10's. This is useful when creating large purchase requisitions and where grouping of items may be convenient.

Account Assignment:

In the column headed with A is where we enter the Account Assignment Code, which is dependent upon the type of purchase being requested. Use the search facility to help you determine which code that you need. There are about 15 Account Assignments you can use. The following list contains the codes you most likely will use:

```
K - Cost Center
A - Asset
P - Project
F - Internal Order
U - Unknown
```

Since we are creating this requisition for training purposes, **we will leave the Account Assignment field blank for simplicity.** Normally you would use K for Cost Center or P for Project. This would then require additional information be entered later to the Item Details section.

Item Category

We can leave this blank. It is used to define how the procurement of the item is controlled. Either Standard, Consignment, Subcontracting etc.

Material

Enter the material number of the requested item in the column headed material. In this case we want to request the purchase of some lumber, item 1006618.

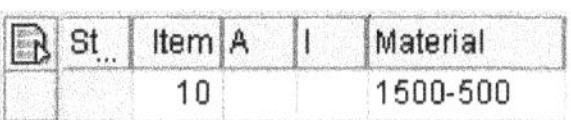

St...	Item	A	I	Material
	10			1500-500

Short Text

Here, enter some short text describing the item; however anything you enter in will be overwritten from the Material Master or Purchasing Information Record. It's helpful to have something in here as you create the requisition to help you keep things organized.

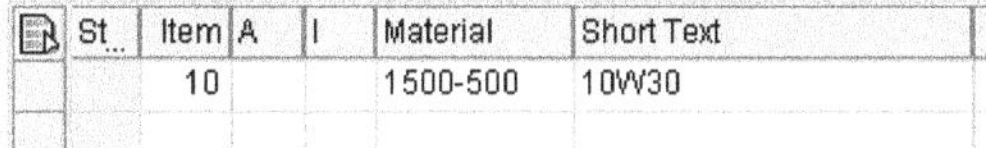

St...	Item	A	I	Material	Short Text
	10			1500-500	10W30

Quantity and Units of Measure

Enter the quantity of the material being requested and indicate the Units of Measure. Ensure that this matches up with the Material Master or an error will appear when you attempt to save the requisition.

St...	Item	A	I	Material	Short Text	Quantity	Unit
	10			1500-500	10W30	200	QT

Delivery Date Category and Delivery Date

You can use the search facility to enter a Delivery Date Category, such as D for day format and then use the calendar search facility to select an appropriate delivery date.

St...	Item	A	I	Material	Short Text	Quantity	Unit	C	Delivery Date
	10			1500-500	10W30	200	QT	D	07/31/09

Material Group

The best place to get the Material Group number is from the Material Master. If you don't have the material group number, open another SAP session, , enter MM03 in the command box to get to the Display Material Master initial screen, enter the material number and enter. On the Purchasing tab you will locate the material group.

St..	Item	A	I	Material	Short Text	Quantity	Unit	C	Delivery Date	Matl Group
	10			1500-500	10W30	200	QT	D	07/31/09	010

Plant

SAP will need a plant for the requisition. We will use plant 3000 in New York.

St..	Item	A	I	Material	Short Text	Quantity	Unit	C	Delivery Date	Matl Group	Plant
	10			1500-500	10W30	200	QT	D	07/31/09	010	3000

Storage Location

Depending upon your systems configuration, SAP may need a storage location. On this training client, it isn't necessary.

St..	Item	A	I	Material	Short Text	Quantity	Unit	C	Delivery Date	Matl Group	Plant	Stor. Loc.
	10			1500-500	10W30	200	QT	D	07/31/09	010	3000	

Purchasing Group

This information is easily found on the Material Master in several different places. If you don't have the Purchasing Group number, open another SAP session, , enter MM03 in the command box to get to the Display Material Master initial screen, enter the material number, the plant and then enter. On the Purchasing tab you will locate the purchasing group.

St..	Item	A	I	Material	Short Text	Quantity	Unit	C	Delivery Date	Matl Group	Plant	Stor. Loc.	PGr
	10			1500-500	10W30	200	QT	D	07/31/09	010	3000		000

Requisitioner

In the requisitioner field, enter your SAP user ID to help identify who created the requisition.

St...	Item	A	I	Material	Short Text	Quantity	Unit	C	Delivery Date	Matl Group	Plant	Stor. Loc.	PGr	Requisnr.
	10			1500-500	10W30	200	QT	D	07/31/09	010	3000		000	Martinez

Tracking

The tracking field is a place for you to enter a unique identification that will help you as an SAP user to find purchase requisitions you created. This is a "free field" allowing any entry. You can use some type of unique name that will group together various requisitions that are in some way related, like 2009OIL, to group requisitions related to 2009 Oil Changes. Using your three initials with the date created MAY be another way for you to find this document in the future.

St...	Item	A	I	Material	Short Text	Quantity	Unit	C	Delivery Date	Matl Group	Plant	Stor. Loc.	PGr	Requisnr.	Tracking...
	10			1500-500	10W30	200	QT	D	07/31/09	010	3000		000	Martinez	2009Oil

Designated Vendor

If you have a vendor in mind that you want to use, or know of the vendor that purchasing will use, you can enter that number here.

St...	Item	A	I	Material	Short Text	Quantity	Unit	C	Delivery Date	Matl Group	Plant	Stor. Loc.	PGr	Requisnr.	Tracking...	Des.Vendor
	10			1500-500	10W30	200	QT	D	07/31/09	010	3000		000	Martinez	2009Oil	7

Another thing we can do if we DO NOT know what vendor to use, we can select the check box next too Source Determination and let SAP select the vendor for us. As of now, we know the vendor we will use, #7, so enter the vendor number and leave this unchecked.

☐ Source Determination

This is all the information we will enter on the Item Overview section. Now select the green check mark or hit Enter. You will notice that some of the fields on the overview have been replaced with different information from the various Master Data in SAP.

St...	Item	A	I	Material	Short Text	Quantity	Unit	C	Delivery Date	Matl Group	Plant	Stor. Loc.	PGr	Requisnr.	Tracking...	Des.Vendor
	10			1500-500	10W30 MOTOR OIL QT.	200	QT	D	07/31/2009	Consumable	New York		000	Martinez	2009OIL	7

Also, the **Item Detail** section can now be opened up.

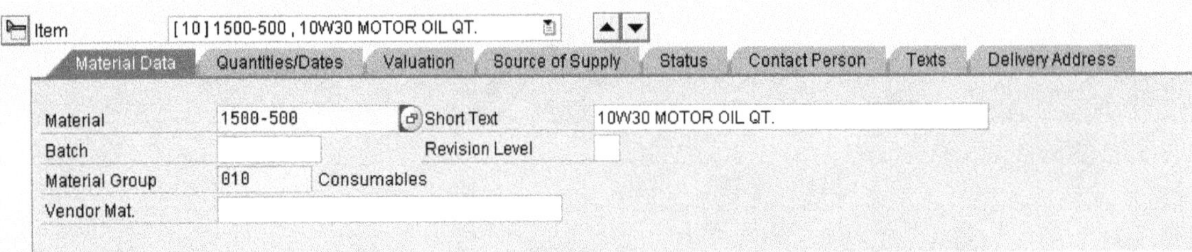

Valuation Price

SAP will require a Valuation Price. This is the price per unit of measure. In this example enter $0.89 per quart. Valuation Price can/should be located in the Material Master and will populate the field automatically if it is present in the Material Master. If not, a search of previous purchase requisitions or orders will be needed to find the latest purchase price.

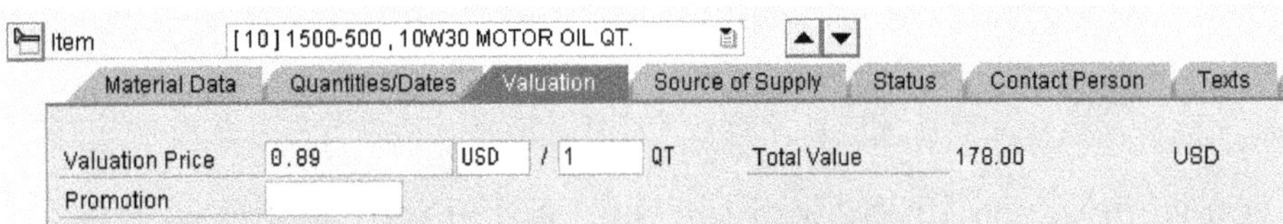

Now we are ready to save the Purchase requisition we have created. Select the SAVE icon .

The Purchase Requisition is created and assigned a requisition number located in the status bar at the bottom. **NOTE:** It may be important for you to remember this number for future reference.

Purchase requisition number 0010013721 created

ME53N Display a Purchase Requisition

Objective: To locate and display a purchase requisition created in SAP. This is especially helpful when trying to locate the latest/last valuation price for a particular material.

SAP Menu Path:

> **Logistics > Materials Management > Purchasing > Purchase Requisition > ME53N - Display**

The **"Display Purchase Req."** screen will come up with the last purchase requisition you created defaulting in. To display a different requisition, or if the requisition didn't come up, select the Other Requisition button and a pop up window appears.

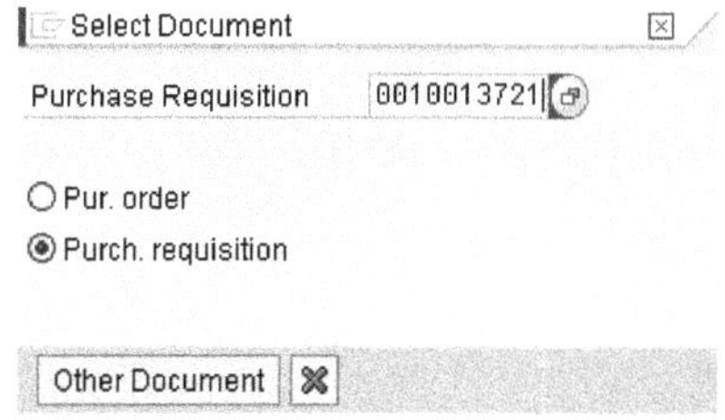

Here you can enter a requisition number in the field. Click on the "Purch. Requisition" radio button if needed and then select the Other Document button to view the Purchase Requisition desired.

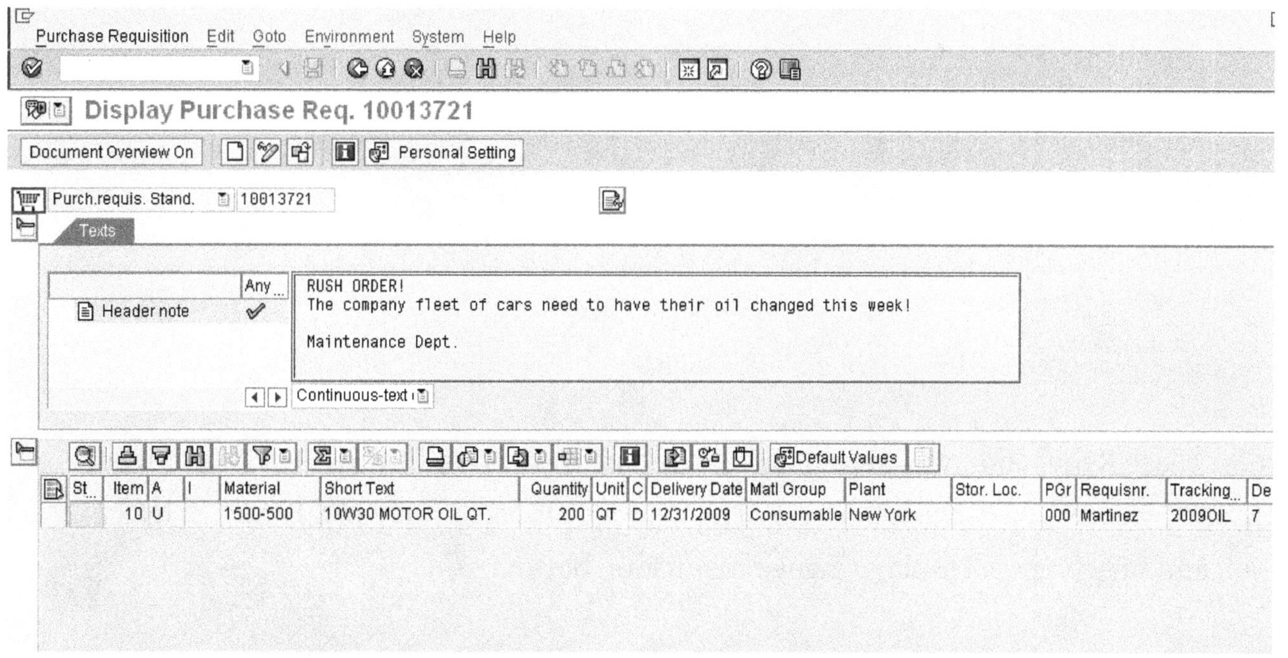

ME52N Changing a Purchase Requisition

Objective: To change an existing purchase requisition that has been entered into SAP.

Purchase Requisitions can be changed or modified as part of the material planning process by an MRP controller. Since SAP can automatically create purchase requisitions for production, as changes in schedules arise, it is important for the MRP controller to keep an eye on purchase requisitions for their corresponding departments.

Manually entered requisitions can also be changed by the user who created the purchase requisition. Any changes **MUST** be made prior to the purchasing department processing the requisition.

SAP Menu Path:

> **Logistics > Materials Management > Purchasing > Purchase Requisition > ME52N - Change**

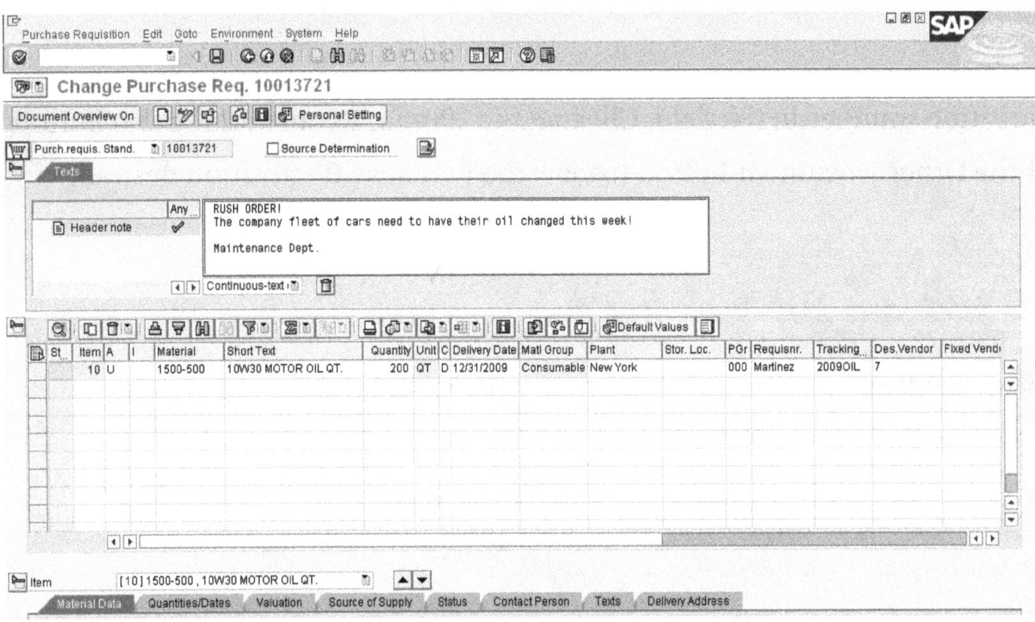

The last Purchase Requisition you were working on comes up in the **Change Purchase Req. XXXXXXXX** screen. You can also get to the change requisition screen when DISPLAYING a requisition and selecting the Display/Change requisition button.

Now that we are in the change screen, we want to change this requisition by adding another item to it. In this case we need to add some 10W40 motor oil to our purchase requisition. We follow the same rules as we did when we initially created the purchase requisition.

The next **Line Item** number is 20.

St..	Item	A	I	Material	Short Text
	10			1500-500	10W30 MOTOR OIL QT.
	20				

The **Account Assignment** in left BLANK!.

St..	Item	A	I	Material	Short Text
	10			1500-500	10W30 MOTOR OIL QT.
	20				

The **Material Number** for the 10W40 is 1500-600 and enter some short text if you wish. It most likely will be overwritten.

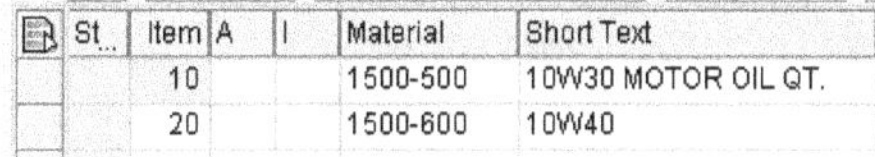

St..	Item	A	I	Material	Short Text
	10			1500-500	10W30 MOTOR OIL QT.
	20			1500-600	10W40

Next enter the **Quantity and Unit of Measurement.**

St..	Item	A	I	Material	Short Text	Quantity	Unit
	10			1500-500	10W30 MOTOR OIL QT.	200	QT
	20			1500-600	10W40	100	QT

Next enter the **Delivery Date Category and Delivery Date.**

St..	Item	A	I	Material	Short Text	Quantity	Unit	C	Delivery Date
	10			1500-500	10W30 MOTOR OIL QT.	200	QT	D	07/31/2009
	20			1500-600	10W40	100	QT	D	07/31/2009

Next we need to enter the **Material Group.** The best place to get the Material Group number is from the Material Master. If you don't have the material group number, open another SAP session, , enter MM03 in the command box to get to the Display Material Master initial screen, enter the material number and plant in the pop up window and then enter. On the Purchasing tab you will locate the material group.

St..	Item	A	I	Material	Short Text	Quantity	Unit	C	Delivery Date	Matl Group
	10			1500-500	10W30 MOTOR OIL QT.	200	QT	D	07/31/2009	Consumable
	20			1500-600	10W40	100	QT	D	07/31/2009	010

ME52N Changing a Purchase Requisition

Next, enter a Plant and Storage Location.

St...	Item	A	I	Material	Short Text	Quantity	Unit	C	Delivery Date	Matl Group	Plant	Stor. Loc.
	10			1500-500	10W30 MOTOR OIL QT.	200	QT	D	07/31/2009	Consumable	New York	
	20			1500-600	10W40	100	QT	D	07/31/2009	010	3000	

Next enter the **Purchasing Group** prior to saving the requisition. This information is easily found on the Material Master in several different places. If you don't have the Purchasing Group number, open another SAP session, , enter MM03 in the command box to get to the Display Material Master initial screen, enter the material number, the plant and then enter. On the Purchasing tab you will locate the purchasing group.

St...	Item	A	I	Material	Short Text	Quantity	Unit	C	Delivery Date	Matl Group	Plant	Stor. Loc.	PGr
	10			1500-500	10W30 MOTOR OIL QT.	200	QT	D	07/31/2009	Consumable	New York		000
	20			1500-600	10W40	100	QT	D	07/31/2009	010	3000		000

Enter your SAP user ID as requisitioner and if you like, enter some tracking ID.

St...	Item	A	I	Material	Short Text	Quantity	Unit	C	Delivery Date	Matl Group	Plant	Stor. Loc.	PGr	Requisnr.	Tracking...
	10			1500-500	10W30 MOTOR OIL QT.	200	QT	D	07/31/2009	Consumable	New York		000	Martinez	2009OIL
	20			1500-600	10W40	100	QT	D	07/31/2009	010	3000		000	Martinez	2009Oil

Enter a designated vendor if you know who the vendor is.

St...	Item	A	I	Material	Short Text	Quantity	Unit	C	Delivery Date	Matl Group	Plant	Stor. Loc.	PGr	Requisnr.	Tracking...	Des.Vendor
	10			1500-500	10W30 MOTOR OIL QT.	200	QT	D	07/31/2009	Consumable	New York		000	Martinez	2009OIL	7
	20			1500-600	10W40	100	QT	D	07/31/2009	010	3000		000	Martinez	2009Oil	7

Now go to the **Item Details** table. SAP requires a Valuation price. Select Line Item 20 and check the Valuations tab to ensure that the price has been pulled in by SAP.

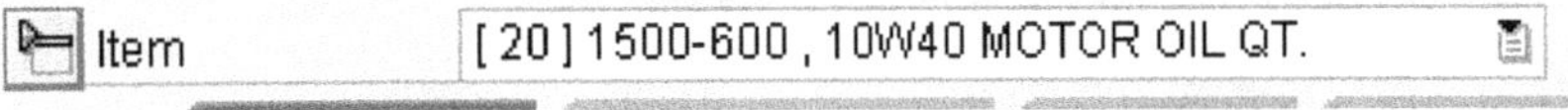

When ready, select the SAVE icon and SAP will note that the Purchase Requisition was changed while keeping the same Purchase Requisition number. Purchase requisition 0010013721 changed

To delete an Item from a purchase requisition, ensure you are in Change mode by selecting the Change icon, highlight the item row and select the icon. A warning will come up saying selected item will be deleted, Select yes and then save the requisition to save the changes.

Purchase Requisition Item Details Section

Now that we have created a Purchase Requisition and changed a purchase requisition, we need to look over the final section of the requisition which is the Item Details section. Using ME53N, display the purchase requisition just created.

SAP Menu Path:

> **Logistics > Materials Management > Purchasing > Purchase Requisition > ME53N – Display**

The last purchase requisition you were working on should default in. If not, enter the purchase requisition number and then enter.

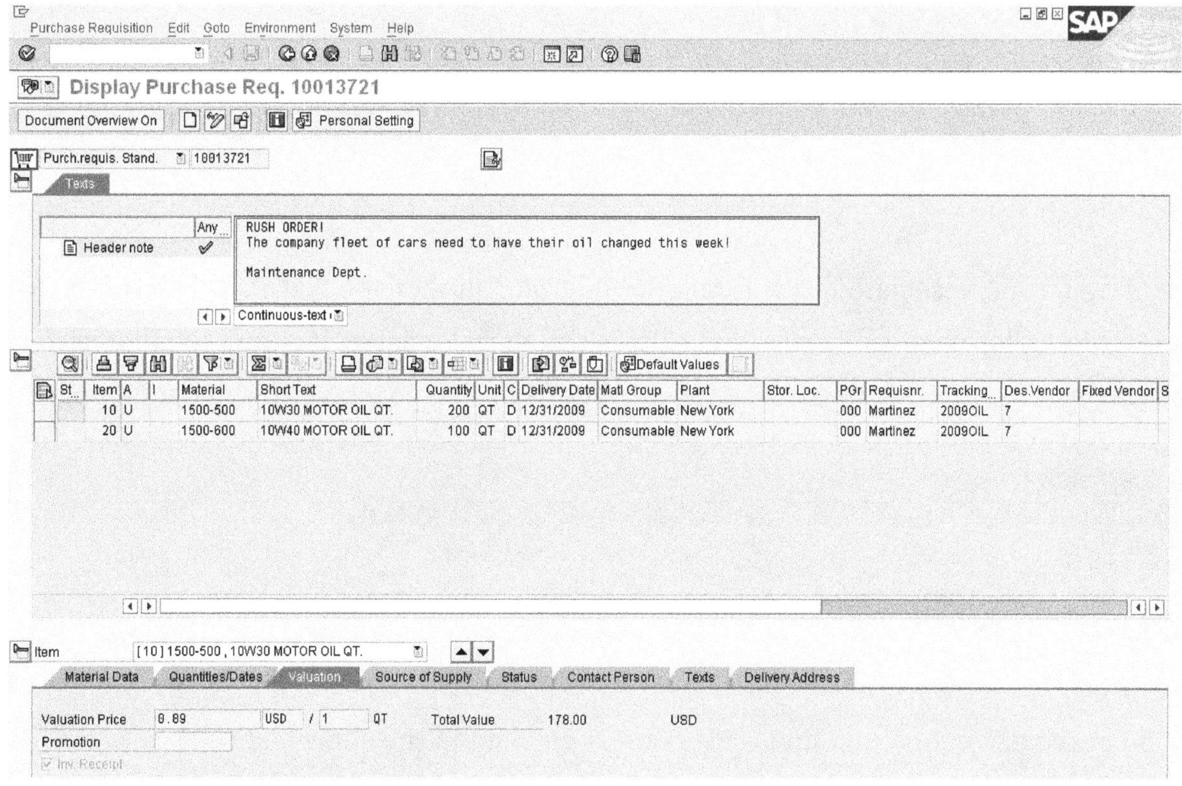

Now we will spend some time reviewing the **Item Details** portion of the requisition. Often, you will need to make entries in this section prior to saving the original purchase requisition. This is particularly true when dealing with specific **Account Assignments** such as cost centers or projects.

Purchase Requisition Item Details Section

The first field in the Item Detail section is the Item Field. This field is linked directly to the items in the purchase requisition. By changing the item in this field, you change what data is displayed in the various tabs.

Item Number 10

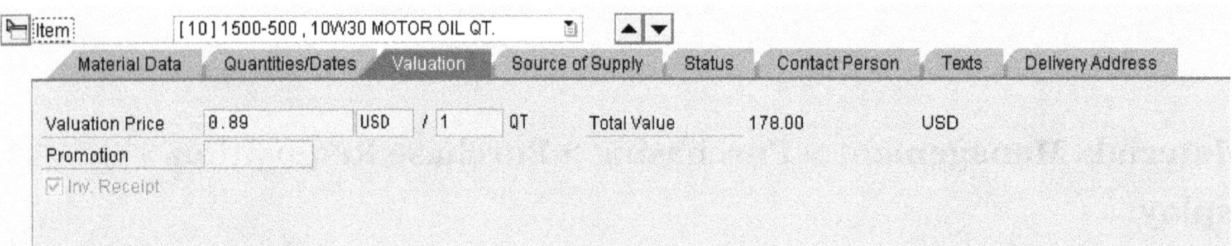

Item Number 20

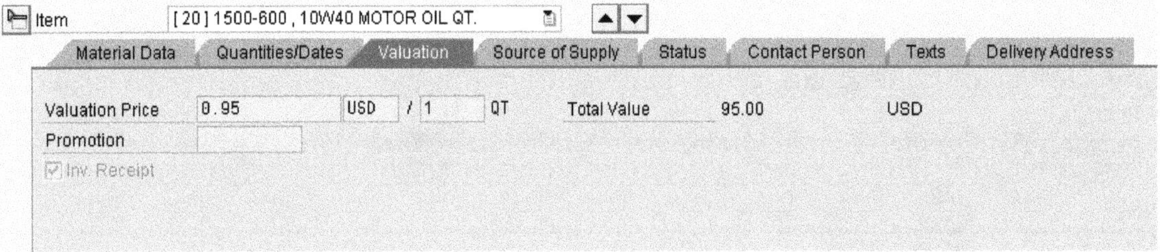

Let's look at the Item Details associated with Item 20, Material Number 1500-600. The first tab is the Material Data tab. This data is directly read from the material master. It shows the material number, and the short text associated with it along with the Material Group with which it belongs.

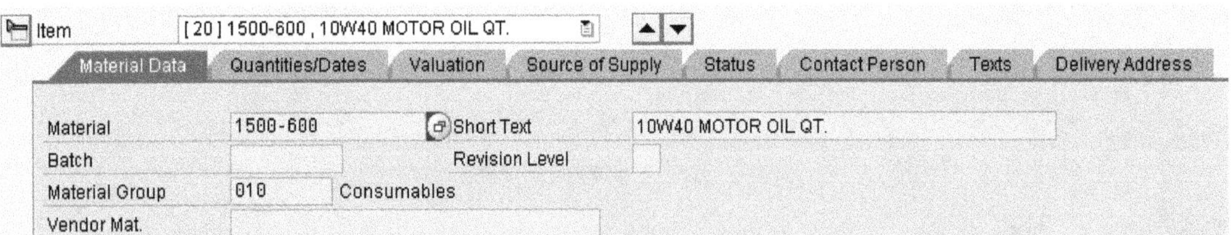

Notice that on the purchase requisition, that if we enter some data in the short text field as well as the material group field, that SAP over wrote what we entered with what the system "prefers" as an entry. It is also possible to enter data here initially as opposed to the Item Overview table.

The next tab we will look at is the **Quantities and Dates** tab.

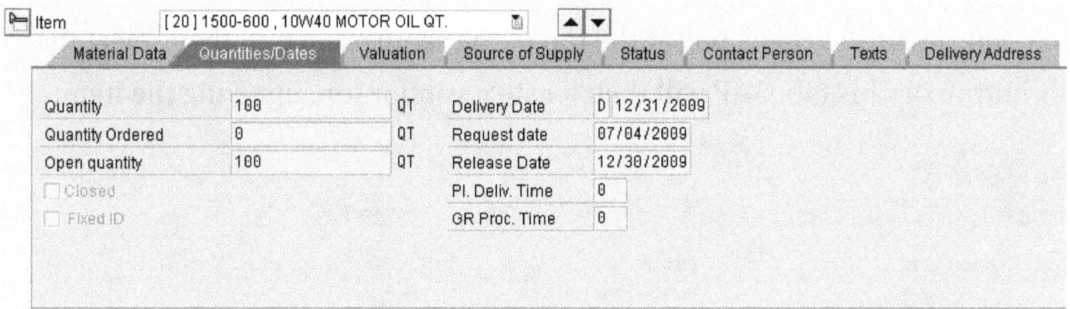

On this tab we can see that we requisitioned 100 quarts of 10W40 oil, but nothing has been ordered and there is an Open Amount of 100 quarts waiting to be filled.

We also see that the Delivery Date that we entered earlier has defaulted in as well as the date we created the purchase requisition.

The next tab we will look at is the Valuation Tab. The **Valuation** Tab is where the value of each individual item is entered and the TOTAL amount of the item is calculated.

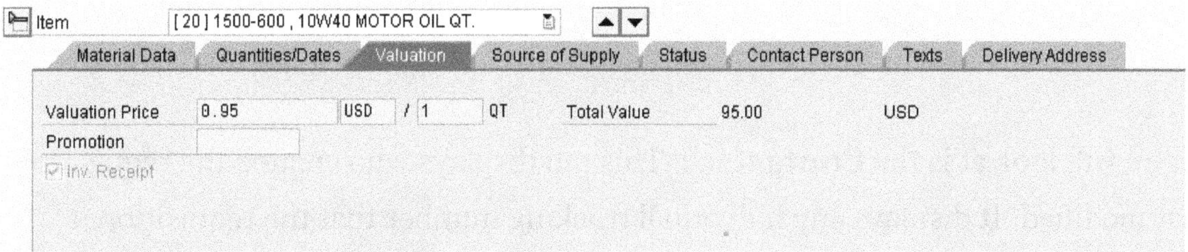

SAP will require you to enter a Valuation for the item you entered in the Item Overview section. You may have entered this in manually earlier OR if the Material Master has been set up properly, the Valuation of the item will default in. You can enter the valuation amount in the Item Details section as well as the Item Overview section. If the Valuation is not available in the Material Master you may need to contact the purchasing department for the latest valuation to enter or try to search for a current requisition that has a valuation entered already. If uncertain, check with the purchasing department for the correct entry.

The next tab we will look at is the **Source of Supply** tab. Here you can also designate who will supply the material being requested OR you can have SAP locate a vendor for you. You do this by first selecting the Source Determination check box at the top of the requisition and then select the Assign Source of Supply button on this tab. SAP will then locate a vendor for supplying the item.

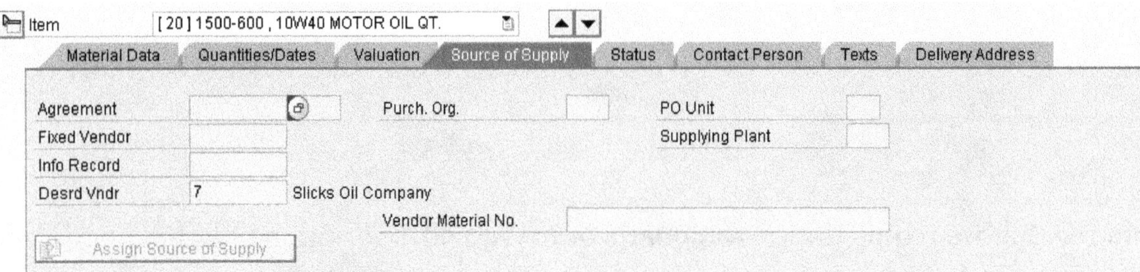

The next tab which we will look at is the **Status** tab. This tab displays the status of the purchase requisition and whether the material has been ordered yet.

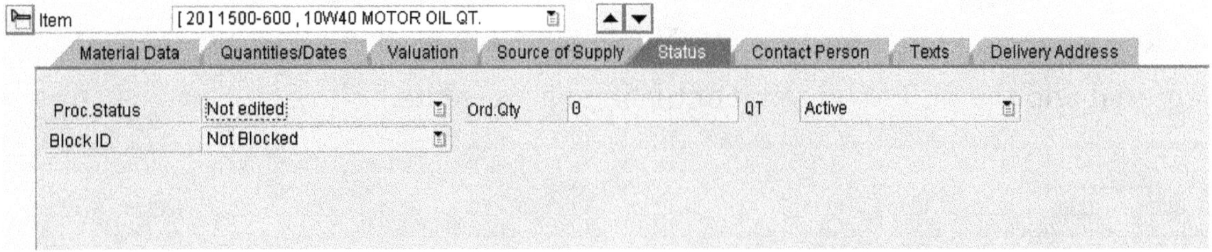

The next tab which we will look at is the **Contact** tab. This tab displays who created the requisition and when it was last modified. It displays any individual tracking number that the requisitioner would like to use and it also displays the Purchasing Group and their contact number.

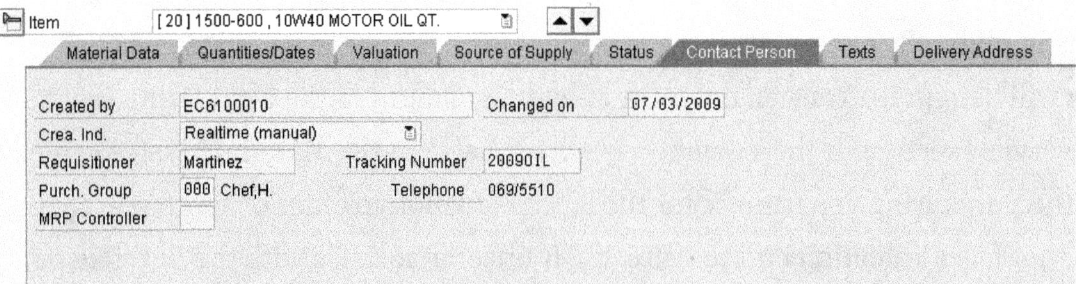

The next tab we will look at is the **Texts** tab. Here you can enter text related to the item, delivery or Material Purchase Order.

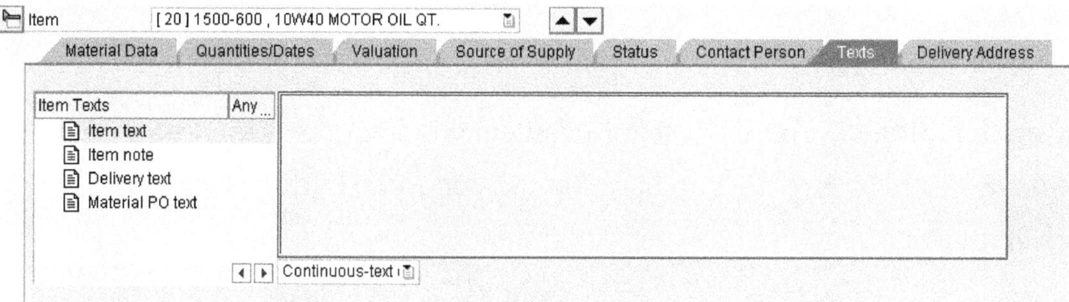

The next tab we will look at is the **Delivery Address** tab. It is important that you check the address out after creating the requisition to ensure that it is going to the correct location.

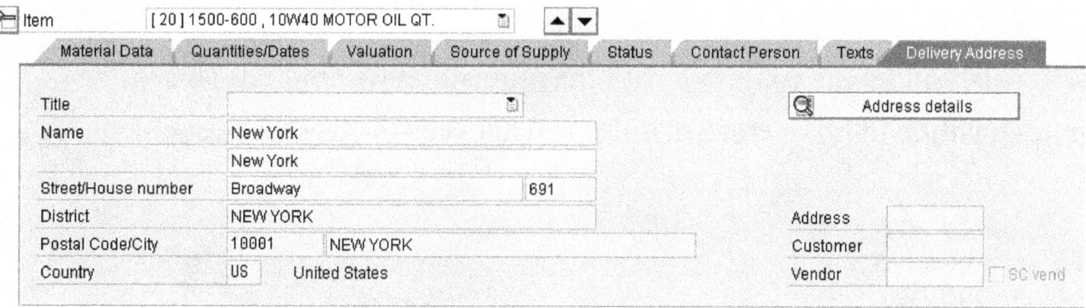

Purchase Requisition Item Details Section

One **IMPORTANT** tab that should appear in the Item Details list is the **Account Assignment tab.** SINCE WE DID NOT ENTER AN ACCOUNT ASSIGNMENT, WE DO NOT HAVE THAT TAB IN OUR ITEM DETAILS. Let's pull up a different purchase requisition to view what that particular tab contains.

Select the Other Requisition button and the Select Document window comes up. Enter requisition number 10002885 and ensure the Purchase Requisition radio button is selected. Then press the Other Document button.

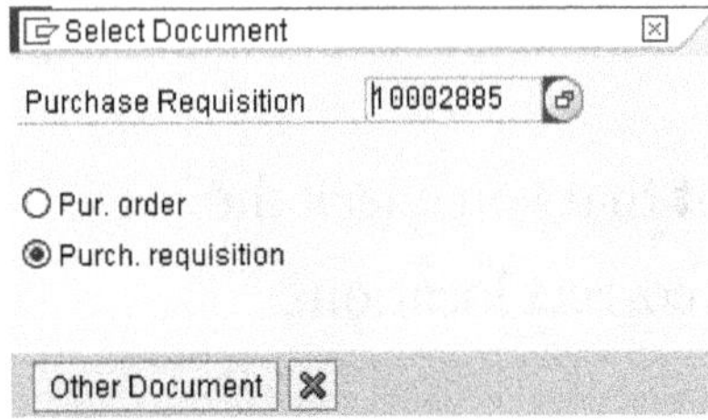

The display purchase requisition screen comes up with the requisition we entered. This is a completely different requisition than we created, but it will allow us to view the Account Assignment tab.

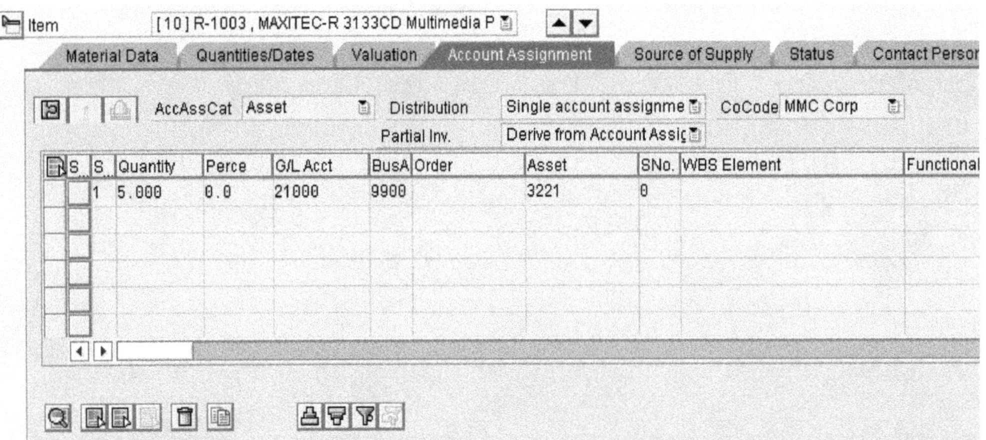

This particular tab is important when you fill out a requisition and are using an Asset Account (A), a Cost Center (K) or one of the other accounts for an Account Assignment. You will need to enter the Account Assignment data in this tab prior to SAP allowing the requisition to be saved.

ME51N Create a Purchase Requisition without a Material Master

Objective: To create a Purchase Requisition for an item without a Material Master record for that item.

When there is **NO Material Master** associated with the item you are creating the Purchase Requisition for, then the requisition will need to have an **Account Assignment** to direct the cost to a specific account. In this way the REQUISITIONER can allocate the costs to the correct accounts. In this training session, we will leave the Account Assignment set at Unknown, however in the business world, you will need to allocate this properly.

SAP Menu Path:

Logistics > Materials Management > Purchasing > Purchase Requisition > ME51N - Create

The **Create Purchase Requisition** screen appears. Start by selecting "Purch. Requis. Stand." in the first field.

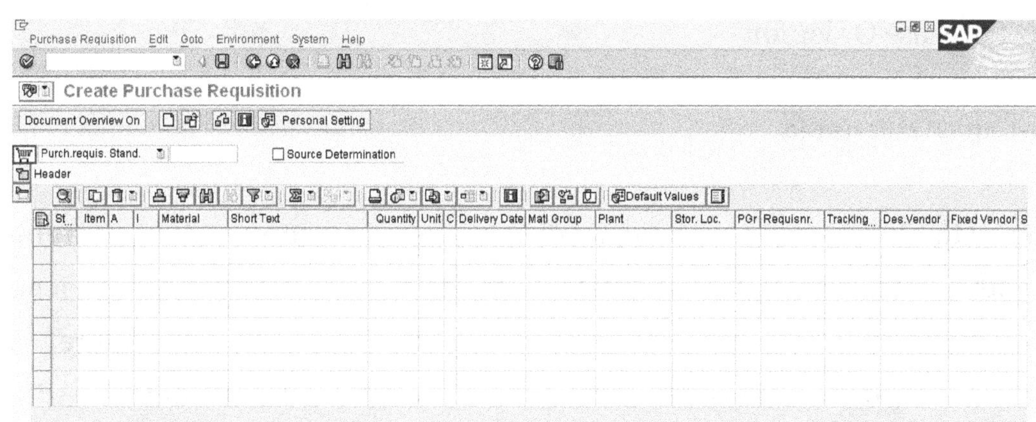

In the Header Text, enter some information regarding the Purchase Requisition without a material master.

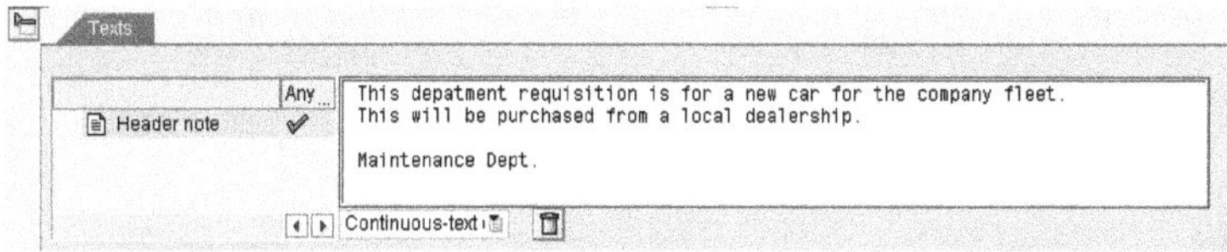

In the detail Line-Item screen, information must be entered since there isn't an existing Material Master record for this purchase requisition to pull information from.

Start with Item Number, Short Text, Quantity, Unit of Measure, Delivery Date Category, Delivery Date, Material Group, Plant, Storage Location, Purchasing Group, Requisitioner, Tracking number if desired.

In the Item Detail on the Valuation Tab, you must enter a Valuation Price.

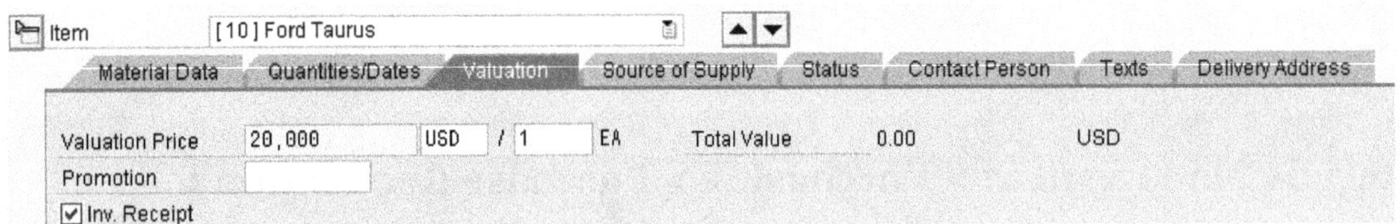

Select the green check mark so SAP will look for errors. If no errors appear, select the SAVE icon and SAP will create the Purchase Requisition even though there was no Material Master for it. Purchasing can now review the requisition and decide what vendor to use to fill the Purchase Requisition and create the Purchase Order for.

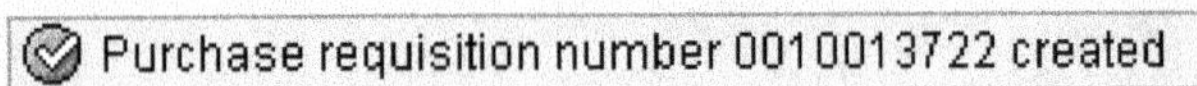

IMPORTANT NOTE: Since this is a training exercise, we did not enter an **Account Assignment** for simplicity. Generally, with a Purchase Requisition you will need to enter an Account Assignment so that the purchasing department knows where to charge the purchase. This in turn will require additional information to be added to the Item Detail section on the Account Assignment tab. SAP will let you know what information it needs prior to creating the purchase requisition.

Purchase Requisition Personal Settings

Objective: To set-up personal settings in the create Purchase Requisition screen. This will help in reducing errors when preparing Purchase Requisitions.

SAP Menu Path:

> **Logistics > Materials Management > Purchasing > Purchase Requisition > ME51N – Create**

The **Create Purchase Requisition** screen comes up.

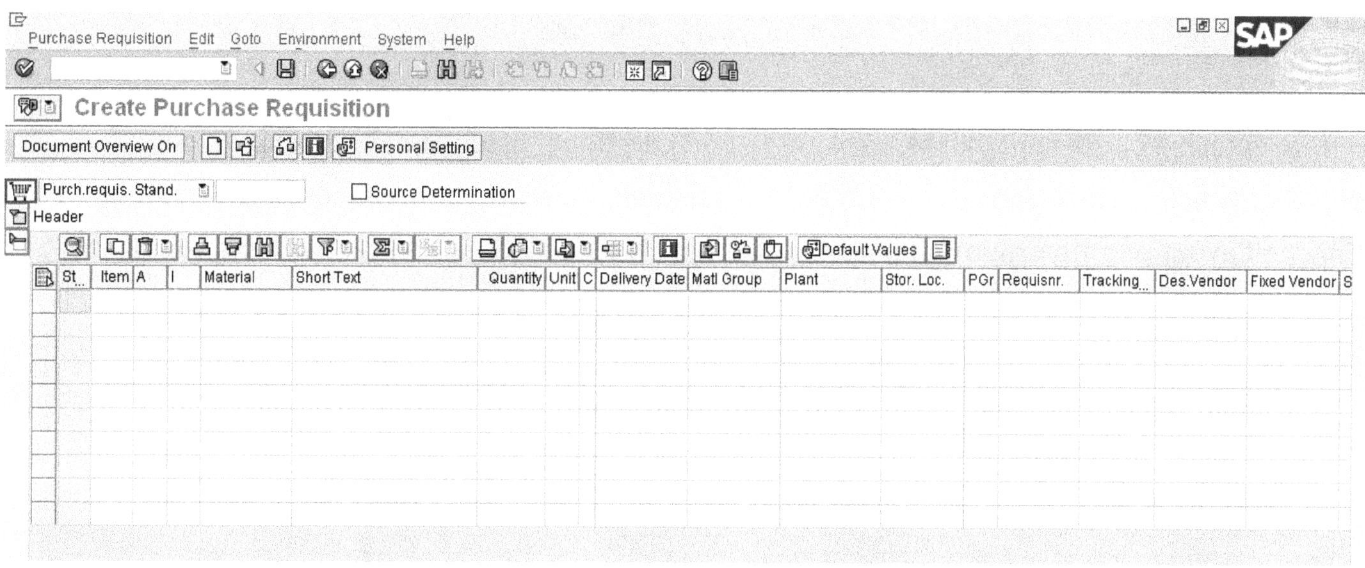

Often times when entering Purchase Requisitions, mandatory fields are not filled in, resulting in SAP error messages and delays. By setting up your personal settings ahead of time, many errors are eliminated.

Purchase Requisition Personal Settings

Click **the Personal** Settings button [Personal setting] to bring up the Personal Settings pop-up window. Select the **Default Values** tab. This is where you set up your personal settings for Purchase Requisition. This will save you time in requisition preparation as well as limit errors when filling out future requisitions.

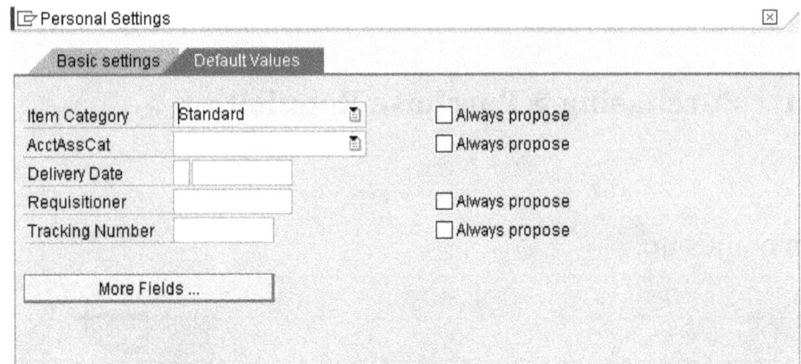

Before entering our default values, we want to add additional fields to have default values populating fields when we create a purchase requisition. Select the More fields button and the Change Layout pop-up window appears.

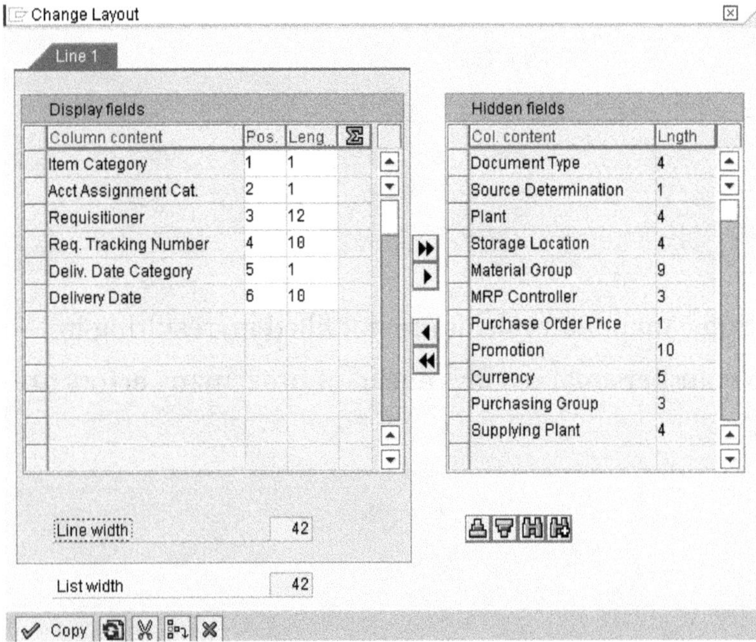

Highlight the fields that you would like to see have default values. In this example, we will add Plant and Purchasing Group.

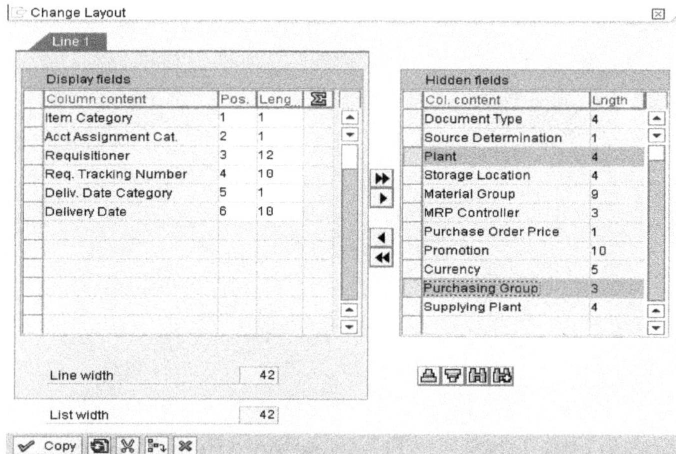

Click on the box next to the Hidden Fields name to highlight the field and then select the black left arrow.

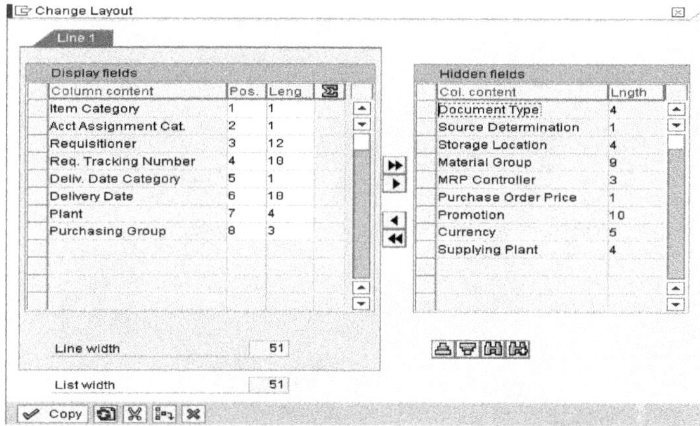

Then select the copy button.

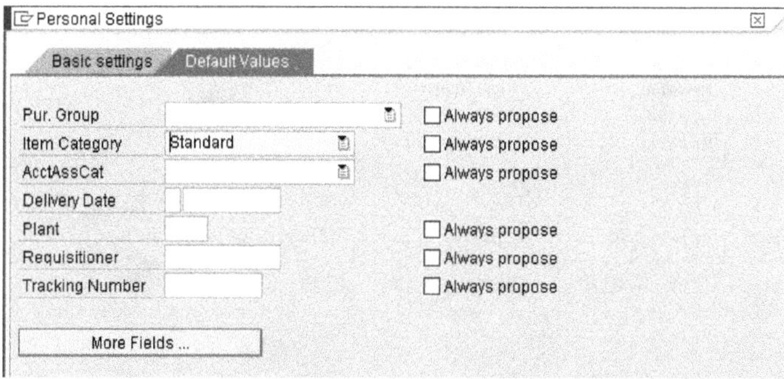

The newly selected fields are now available in the Personal Settings window.

Now you can select the default values you wish to see populate your purchase requisitions every time you begin to create a purchase requisition.

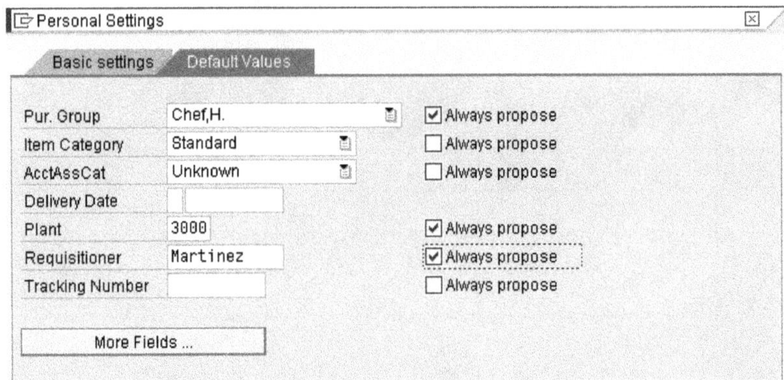

After entering your selections, select the Always Propose check box and then select the SAVE icon [save icon].

Notice now that the purchase requisition now has all the default values you have just selected.

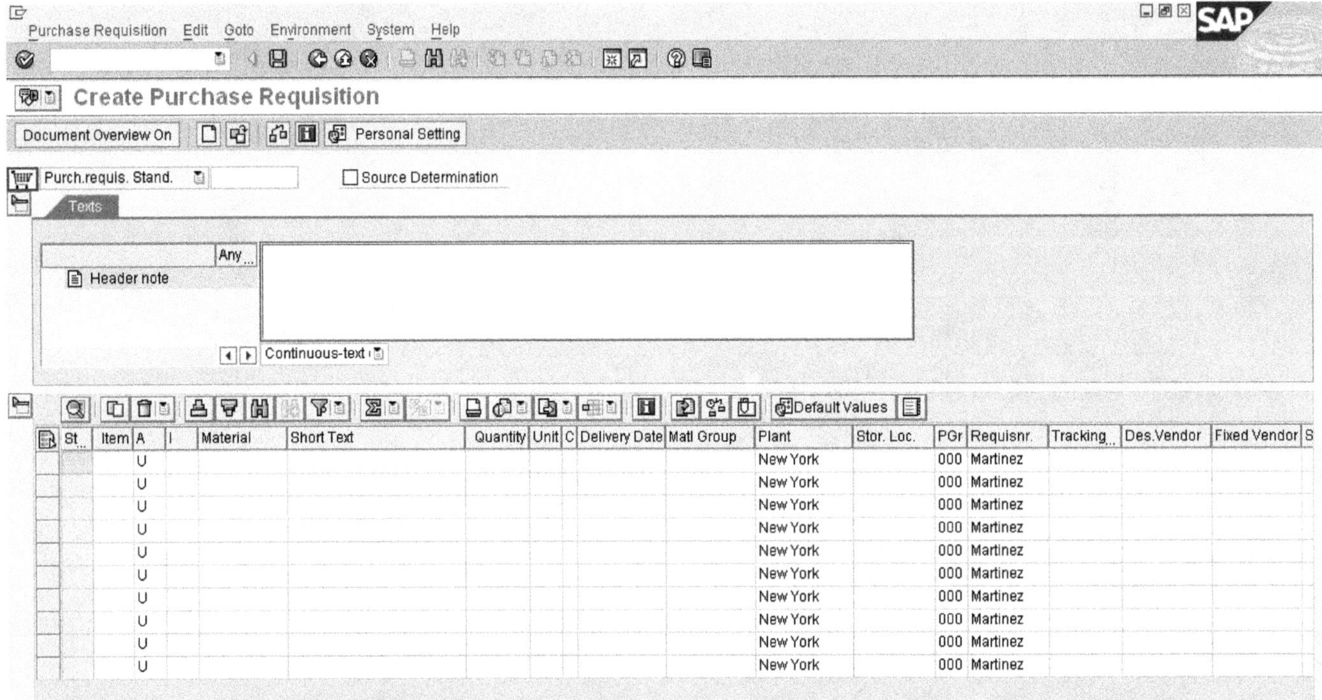

ME5A Purchase Requisition List Display

Objective: To display a list of purchase requisitions and to choose and view an individual purchase requisition from that list display.

SAP Menu Path:

> **Logistics > Materials Management > Purchasing > Purchase Requisition > List Displays > ME5A - General**

The **List Display of Purchase Requisitions** selection screen comes up. Here we can enter various criteria to see a specific list of Purchase Requisitions. Since we set up our Purchase requisitions to have a Delivery Date of July 31, 2009, we can simply use delivery date criteria to view our requisitions. This allows for a very specific list to be created.

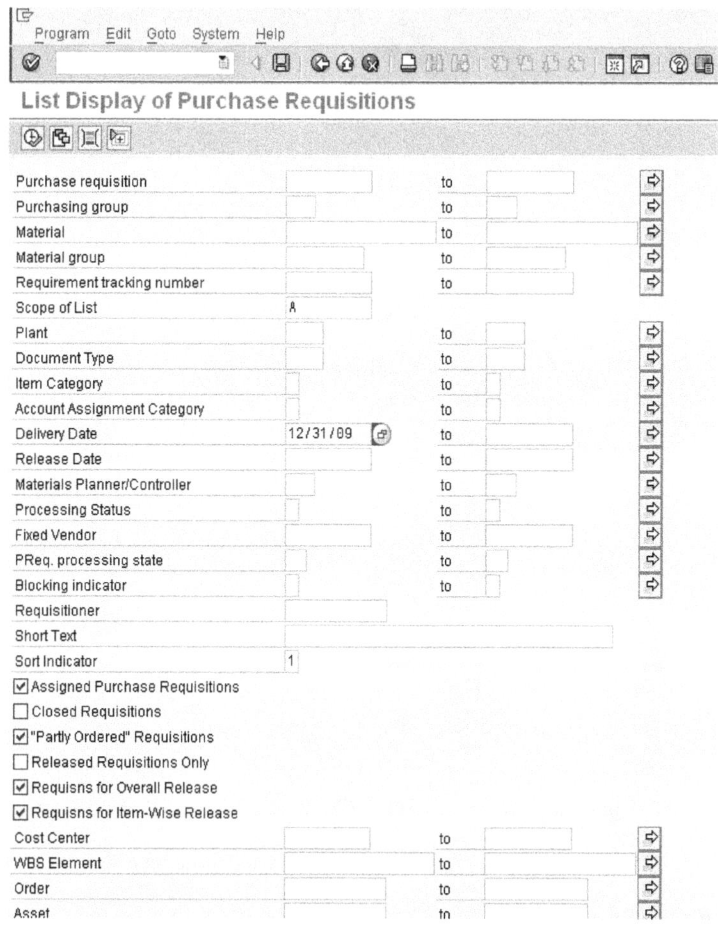

After entering the delivery date, simply select Execute.

A **List Display** of all requisitions created with July 31st, 2009 delivery date appears.

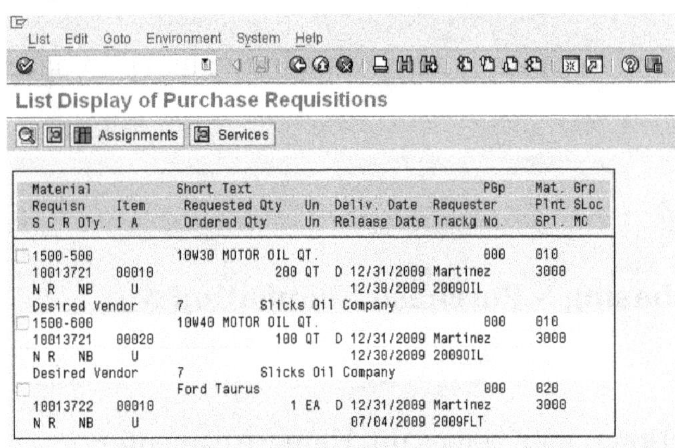

Double click on a requisition number, such as 10013721, and the corresponding requisition will open up.

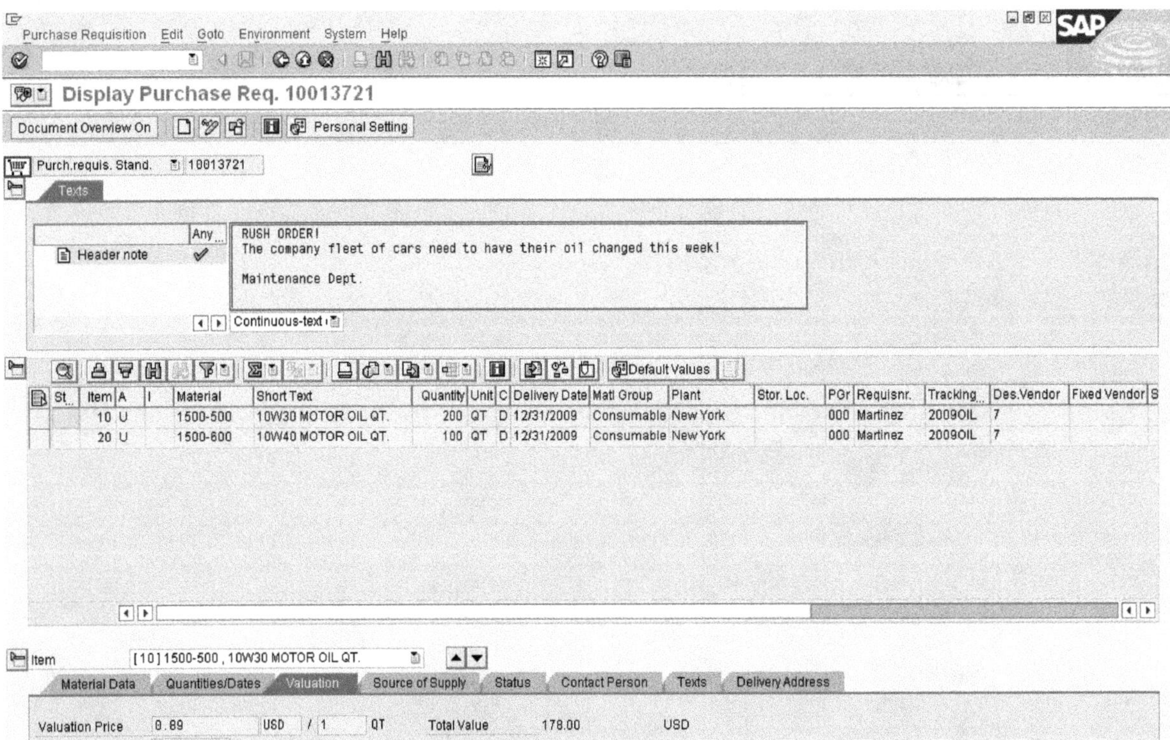

This is particularly useful when you need to locate the latest **Valuation Price.** Since SAP will not allow you to create a purchase requisition without a valuation price, often you will need to search for recent purchase requisitions or purchase orders to locate the price.

For example we want to locate the price of material EKH-013, a 21 Inch Flat Screen Monitor.

Using t-code ME5A, open the **List Display of Purchase Requisitions** selection screen and enter material number EKH-013. **Also select all of the possible check boxes for various purchase requisition statuses. This increases the list to include closed requisitions.**

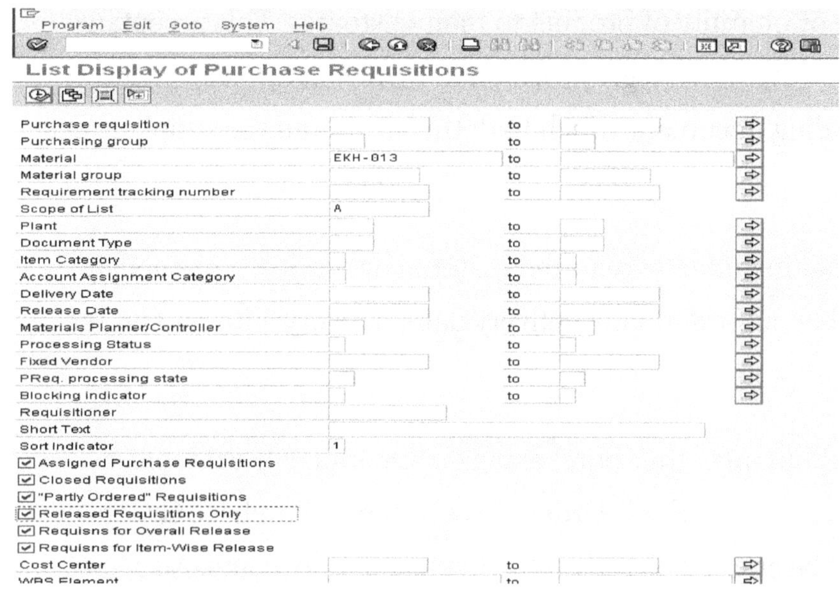

And then Execute the selection screen.

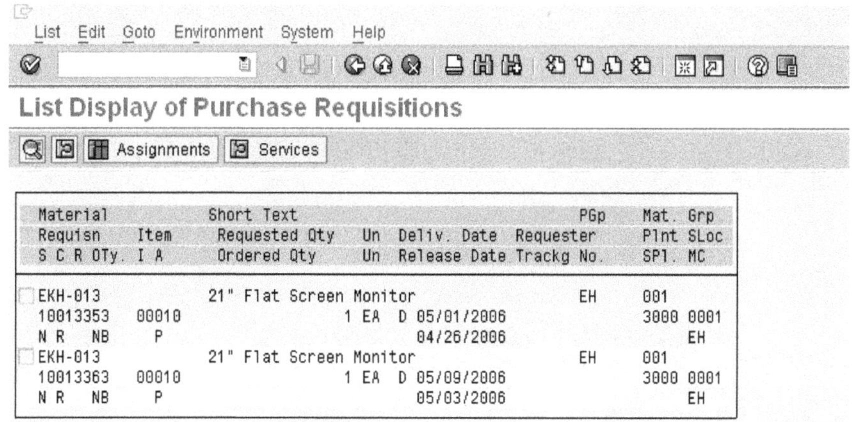

Select the purchase requisition number 10013353 and search for the valuation price on the Valuation Tab in the Item Detail table. The price is $500.00 and can be used the Valuation Price in additional requisitions when the price isn't located in the Material Master.

The Purchase Order

A Purchase Order is a document created by a purchasing department that is sent to a supplier indicating their intent to buy a certain service or amount of product from the supplier. It is used as a communication document between the buyer and supplier. When a supplier accepts the Purchase Order, they agree to supply the service or quantity of product to their customer. This acceptance between a buyer and supplier, depending upon the legal jurisdiction involved, can lead to the Purchase Order becoming a legally binding document which both the buyer and the supplier must honor.

The Purchase Order contains details that include the required material or service, a previously agreed to price, a purchase order number, an order date, delivery date, delivery address and the terms of sale.

The Purchase Order can be created without any other purchasing documents. For example, a Purchase Requisition isn't needed to create a Purchase Order. Departmental Purchase Orders or Price Agreement Purchase Orders may be created directly by individual departments. Also, creating Purchase Orders directly is often the case with complex and detailed purchasing activities.

Purchase Order User Settings

Objective: To set-up personal settings in the create Purchase Order screen. This should help in reducing errors when preparing PO's.

SAP Menu Path:

> **Logistics > Materials Management > Purchasing > Purchase Order > Create > ME21N – Vendor/Supplying Plant Known**

The **Create Purchase Order** screen comes up.

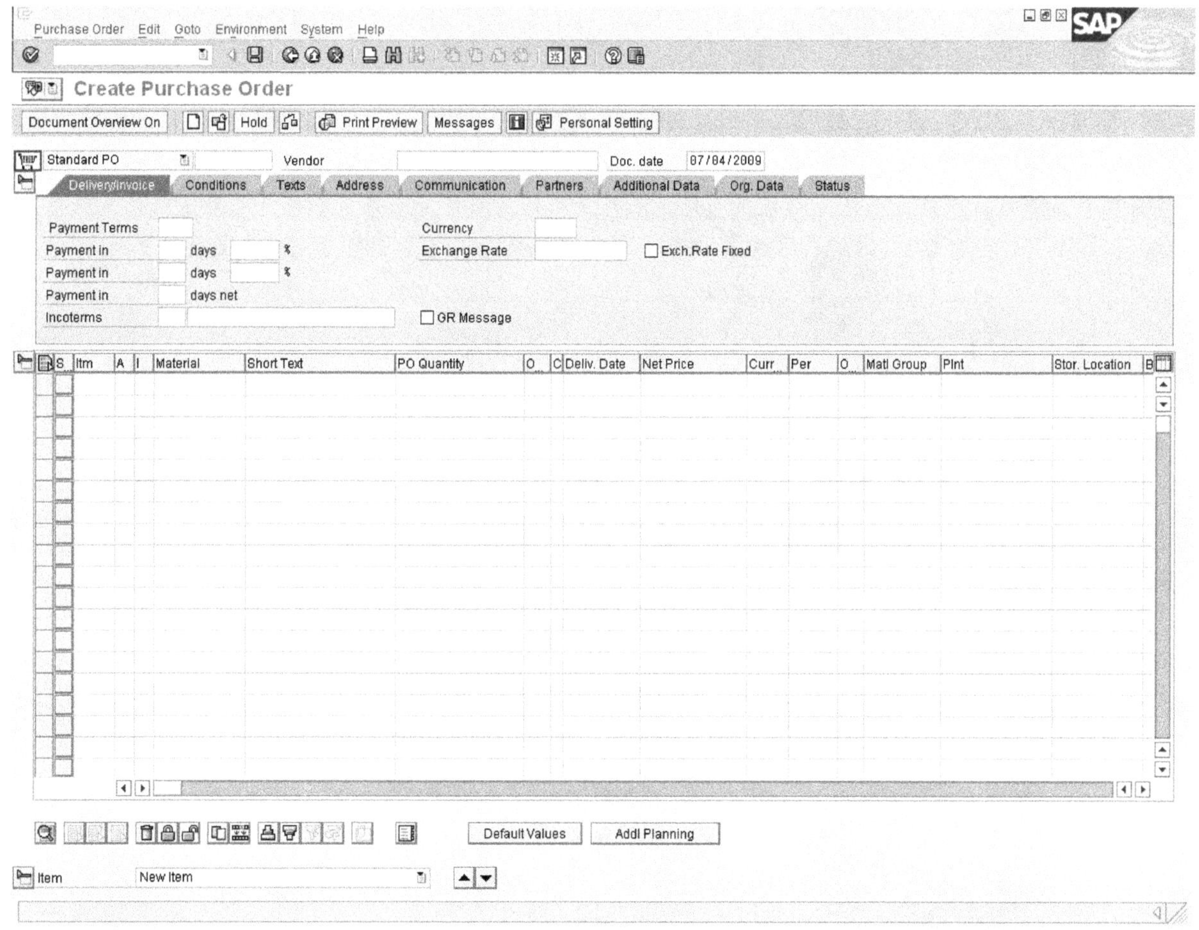

Often times when entering Purchase Orders, mandatory fields are not filled in, resulting in SAP error messages and delays. By setting up your personal settings ahead of time, many errors are eliminated.

Click the **Personal Settings** button [Personal setting] to bring up the Personal Settings pop-up window. Select the **Default Values** tab. This is where you set up you personal Purchase Order defaults both for the **Purchase Order Header** and the **Purchase Order Item** data.

Begin entering the **PO Header** defaults you wish to have automatically entered. In general, purchasing departments will create **Standard PO's,** so we'll set that default for the Document type. Often there is only one Purchasing Organization to choose, so we can default that in. We have several Purchasing groups to choose from. Pick the buyer whom you feel will be responsible for most of the Departmental Purchase Orders you create. And in company code, enter your company code.

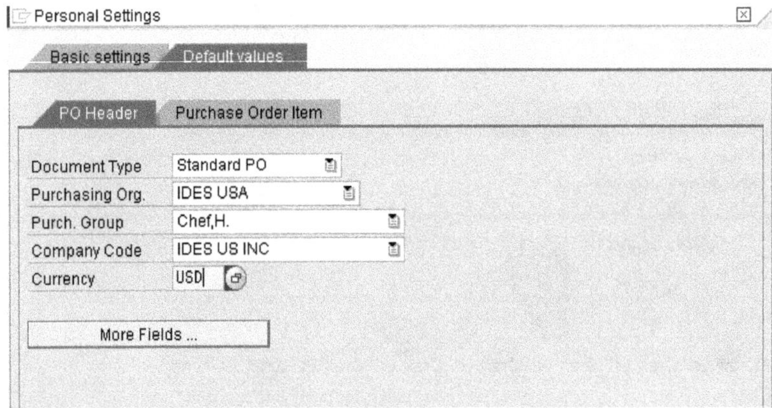

Select the More Fields button to check if there are additional fields that you would like populated for the PO Header data.

Next select the PO item tab. Here you have several other fields, which you can have automatically populated, such as the Plant you work at or Requisitioner field. Select the Always Propose check box next to the fields you've entered.

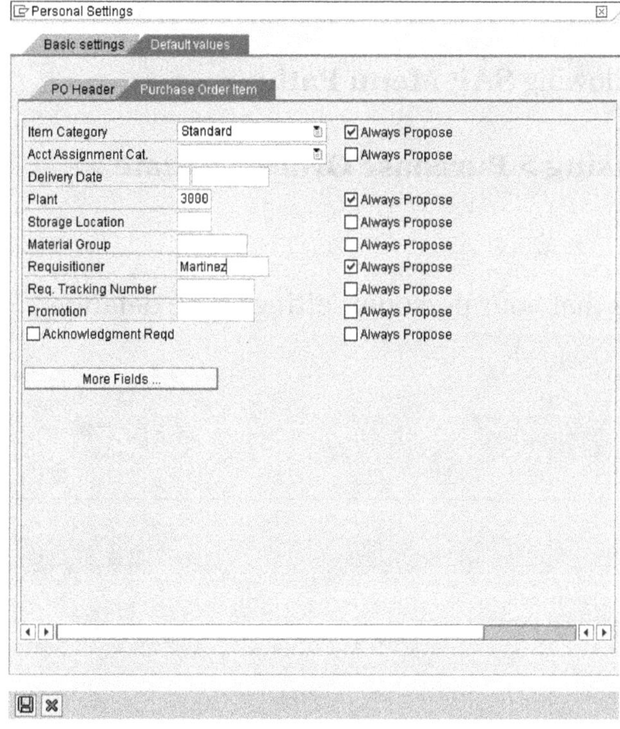

Select the More Fields button to check if there are additional fields that you would like populated for the PO Item data.

When done select the **SAVE** icon on the **Personal Settings** pop-up window. Now whenever you create a new Purchase Order, some of the mandatory fields are populated for you.

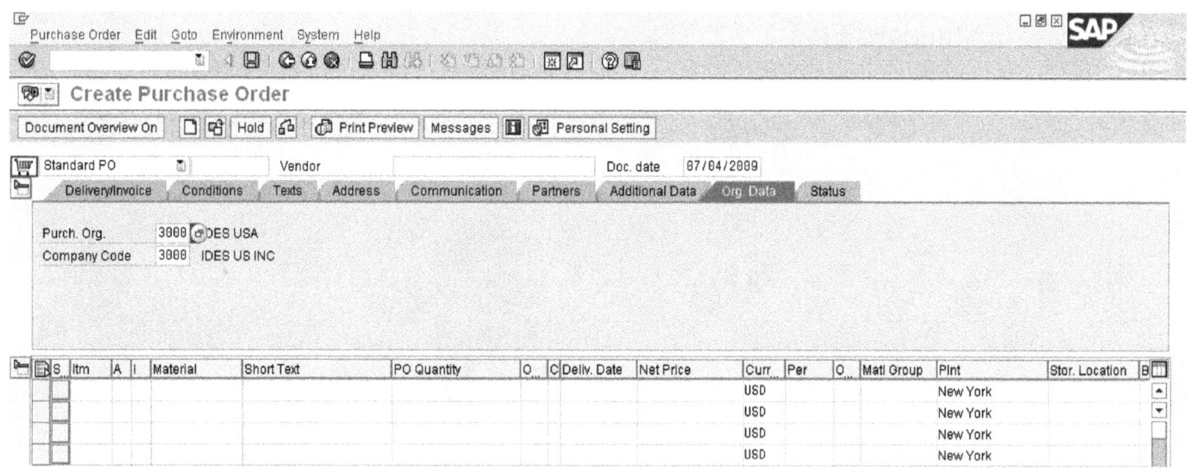

ME21N Creating a Standard Purchase Order

Objective: To create a Departmental Purchase Order directly and skip the creation of a Purchase Requisition.

To create a **Standard Purchase Order,** follow the following **SAP Menu Path:**

> **Logistics > Materials Management > Purchasing > Purchase Order > Create > ME21N Vendor/Supplying Plant Known**

The **Create Purchase Order** screen comes up. Notice that your personal settings have defaulted into the Create Purchase Order screen.

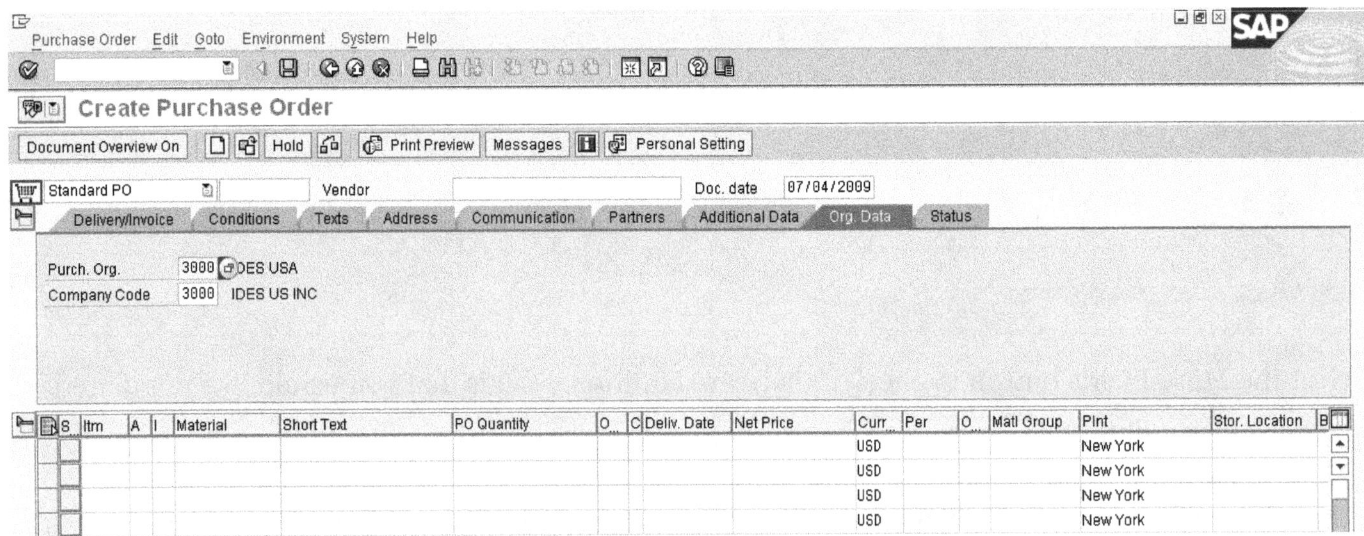

Since we are creating a Standard Purchase Order, ensure that the correct type of purchase order has been selected. In this case, a Standard PO Standard PO.

For a Standard Purchase Order, a vendor must be entered. A vendor number must exist for the propose vendor PRIOR to creating any purchasing document. In this example we will enter vendor number #7. Vendor 7 Slicks Oil Company .

Like a Purchase Requisition, the Purchase Order creation screen is divided into three sections, the ***Purchase Order Header,*** the ***Purchase Order Item Overview*** and the ***Purchase Order Item Detail*** sections. All three sections can be expanded or collapsed by selection of the corresponding section icons .

The Purchase Order Header Section:

Expand the header section and select the Org. Data tab.

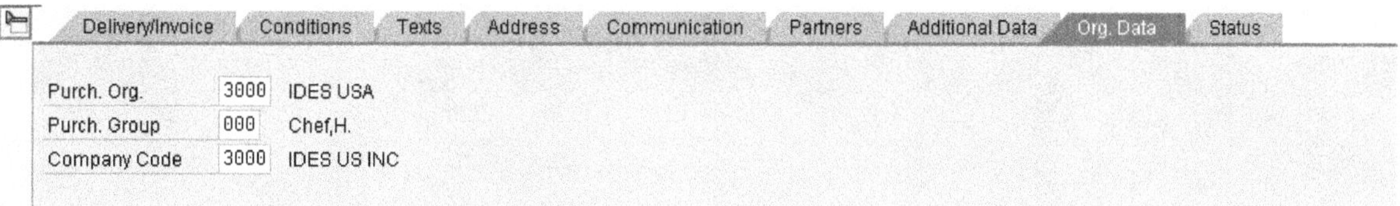

If you have set up your personal purchase order settings, then the Purchasing Org, the Purch. Group and Company Code should have defaulted in. If not, or if you want to change them, enter the correct information.

The Purchase Order Item Overview Section:

Next, select the Item Overview button which opens up a Purchase Order table where we can enter information about the materials being requested.

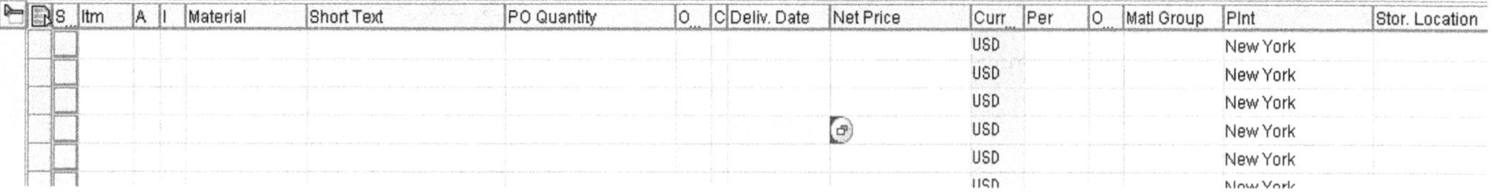

Item Numbering:

On the first row of the table, we will enter the first item requested. In the column headed Item, we begin numbering our items. It is suggested that you number items by 10's.

S	Itm	A	I	Material	Short Text	PO Quantity	O...	C	Deliv. Date	Net Price	Curr	Per	O...	Matl Group	Plnt	Stor. Location	B
	10										USD				New York		
											USD				New York		

Account Assignment:

In the column headed with A is where we enter the Account Assignment Code, which is dependant upon the type of purchase being requested. Use the search facility to help you determine which code you need. There are about 15 Account Assignments you can use. The following list contains the codes you most likely will use:

```
K – Cost Center
A – Asset
P – Project
F – Internal Order
U – Unknown
```

For this exercise we will leave the account assignment blank for simplicity. Addition of an Account Assignment will require additional data in the Item Details section.

S	Itm	A	I	Material	Short Text	PO Quantity	O...	C	Deliv. Date	Net Price	Curr	Per	O...	Matl Group	Plnt	Stor. Location	B
	10	U									USD				New York		

Item Category

We can leave this blank. It is used to define how the procurement of the item is controlled. Either Standard, Consignment, Subcontracting etc.

Material

Enter the material number of the requested item in the column headed material. In this case we want to request the purchase of some fiber cable, item 1018049.

S	Itm	A	I	Material	Short Text	PO Quantity	O...	C	Deliv. Date	Net Price	Curr	Per	O...	Matl Group	Plnt
	10			1500-700							USD				New York
											USD				New York

Short Text

Here, enter some short text describing the item; however anything you enter in here will most likely be overwritten from the Material Master or Purchasing Info Record. It's helpful to have something in here as you create the order to help you keep things organized.

S	Itm	A	I	Material	Short Text	PO Quantity	O	C	Deliv. Date	Net Price	Curr	Per	O	Matl Group	Plnt	Stor. Lo
	10			1500-700	10W50						USD				New York	
											USD				New York	
											USD				New York	

Quantity and Units of Measure

Enter the quantity of the material being requested and indicate the Units of Measure. Ensure that this matches up with the Material Master or an error will appear when you attempt to save the purchase order. Remember when entering a quantity, not to order more than allowed by Departmental Purchase Order rules.

S	Itm	A	I	Material	Short Text	PO Quantity	O	C	Deliv. Date	Net Price	Curr	Per	O	Matl Group	Plnt
	10			1500-700	10W50	100	QT				USD				New York
											USD				New York

Delivery Date Category and Delivery Date

You can use the search facility to enter a Delivery Date Category, such as D for day format and then use the calendar search facility to select an appropriate delivery date. Try to use the vendors delivery date information whenever possible.

S	Itm	A	I	Material	Short Text	PO Quantity	O	C	Deliv. Date	Net Price	Curr	Per	O	Matl
	10			1500-700	10W50	100	QT	D	12/31/09		USD			
											USD			
											USD			
											USD			

Net Price

The net price is the per unit price. If a purchasing info record exists, the net price will be taken from it. If you enter a price, it will be overwritten if the info record exists.

Plant

SAP will need a plant for the order. If you have set up your personal settings, this should default in. We will use plant 3000, New York.

Storage Location

SAP will need a storage location. This is the Ship To address. Use the search facility to help select an appropriate location for the item to be stored.

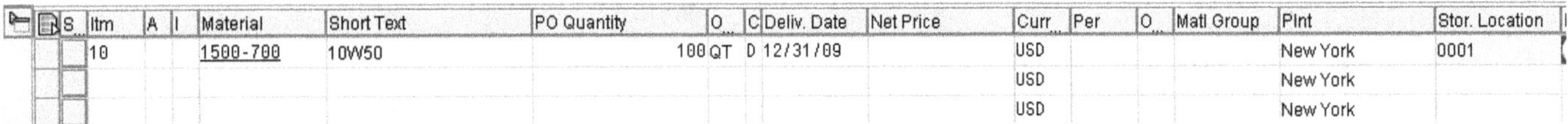

S	Itm	A	I	Material	Short Text	PO Quantity	O..	C	Deliv. Date	Net Price	Curr..	Per	O..	Matl Group	Plnt	Stor. Location
	10			1500-700	10W50	100	QT	D	12/31/09		USD				New York	0001
											USD				New York	
											USD				New York	

Now we will go to the last section, the Item Detail section. Check the delivery address to verify that the correct address is present.

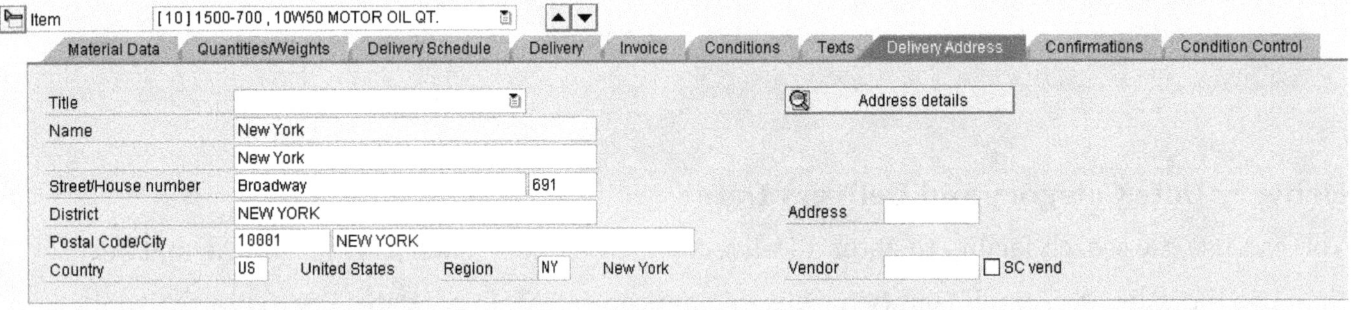

After entering the data, select the green check to look for errors, and then **SAVE** to save the Departmental Purchase Order.

Standard PO created under the number 4500017315

MD04 Create a Purchase Order from a Purchase Requisition

Objective: To create a Purchase Order from a Purchase requisition already created.

We previously created a couple of Purchase Requisitions, 0010013721 & 0010013722. Use t-code ME5A to find those requisitions. In this exercise, we will convert one of these to a Purchase Order.

SAP Menu Path:

> **Logistics > Materials Management > Material Requirements Planning > MRP > Evaluations > MD04 - Stock Requirements List**

The **Stock/Requirements List: Initial Screen** comes up.

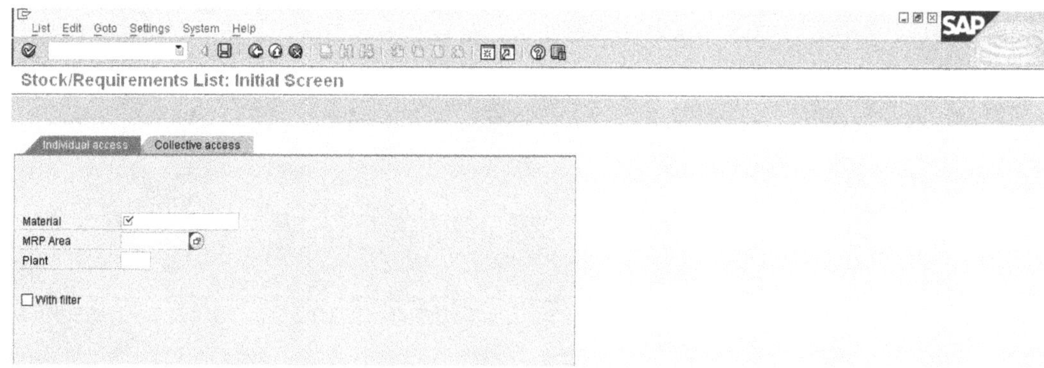

Here we enter a material number and Plant to see if there are any outstanding Purchase Requisitions for the material. A **Stock Requirements List** appears for the material and plant entered.

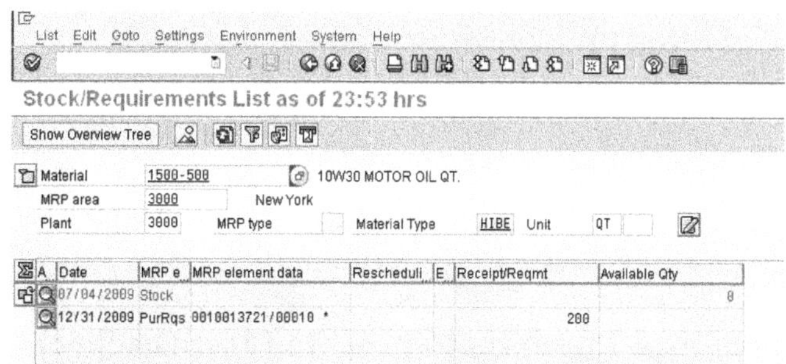

Find the **Purchase Requisition** desired. We see that the requisition we created earlier, 0010013721 is in the column titled "MRP element data".

MD04 Create a Purchase Order from a Purchase Requisition

Select the Element Details icon at the beginning of the row for the requisition desired and the Additional Data for MRP Element pop-up window appears.

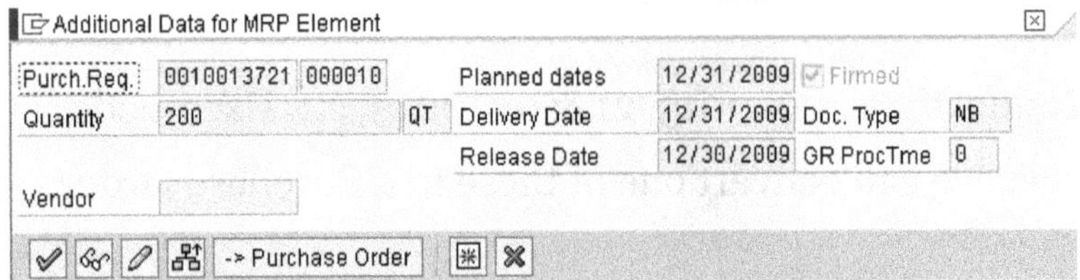

We can now convert the **Purchase Requisition** to a **Purchase Order** by selecting the Purchase Order button -> Purchase Order. **This opens the Create Purchase Order screen.**

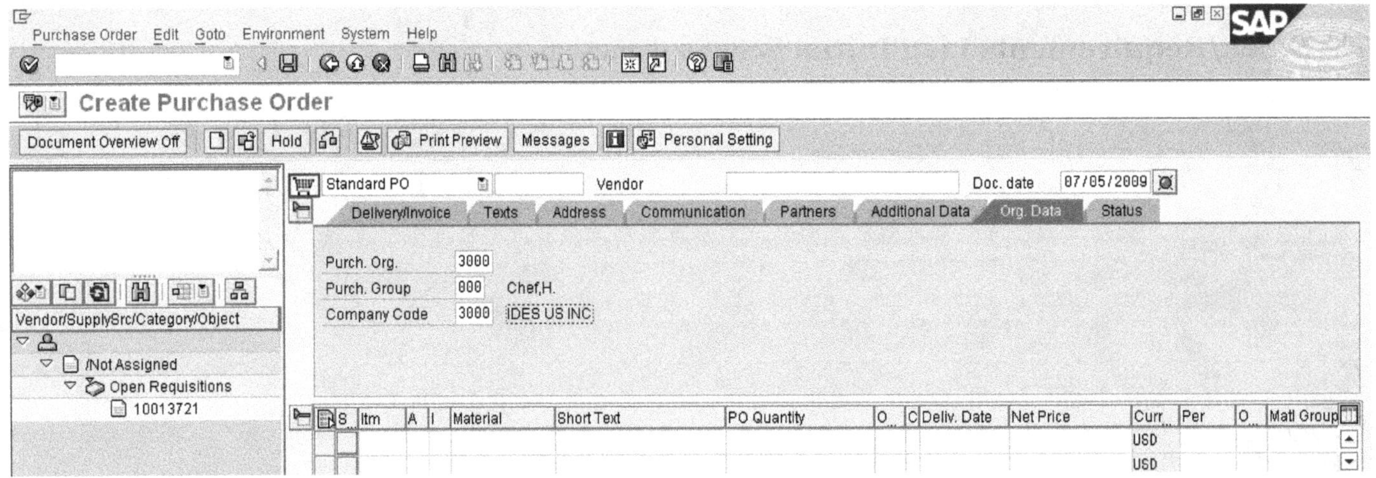

Highlight the **Purchase Requisition Number** in the Object window on the left and then **ADOPT ICON** to populate the order fields. Then select Doc. Overview Off to see only Purchase Order. Select Item Details Icon to verify order details such as delivery date, cost etc.

Click the **SAVE** icon and Purchase order has now been created and an order number assigned. **NOTE:** It may be important for you to remember this number for future reference.

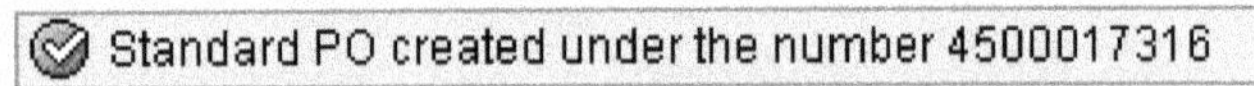

You can now go back to the SAP menu, and enter t-code ME5A Purchase Requisition List Display to find that your requisition is no longer listed since it has been converted to a PO.

Purchase Order Document Overview

Objective: To use the Document Overview to search and select purchasing documents, specifically PO's, to view details regarding that document. This is also a convenient way of creating a NEW PO by copying data from an existing PO.

SAP Menu Path:

> **Logistics > Materials Management > Purchasing > Purchase Order > Create> ME21N – Vendor/Supplying Plant Known**

The **Create Purchase Order** screen comes up.

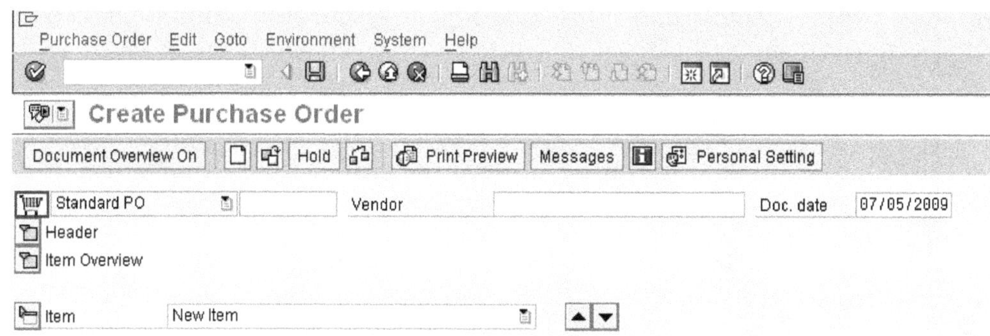

Select the **Document Overview** on button [Document Overview On] and then click the Selection variant icon (three colored diamonds icon). A list of Purchasing Document types comes up which you can use to copy into the new Purchase Order.

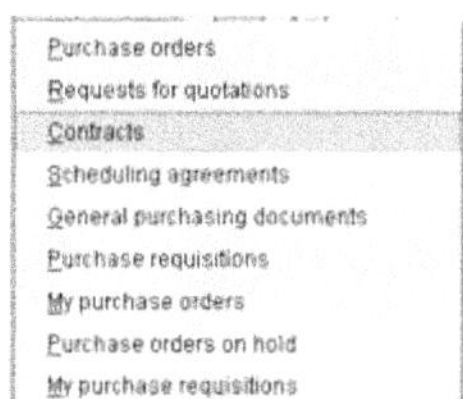

You can select PO others have created as well as yourself by selecting **Purchase orders** from the Document Overview.

The **Purchasing Documents** selection screen comes up. This allows you to find purchase orders by entering in specific criteria. In this example, we enter **Material** number 1500-500 (10W30 Oil) for Plant 3000 (New York). You can always add more information to narrow down your search if the list becomes too large.

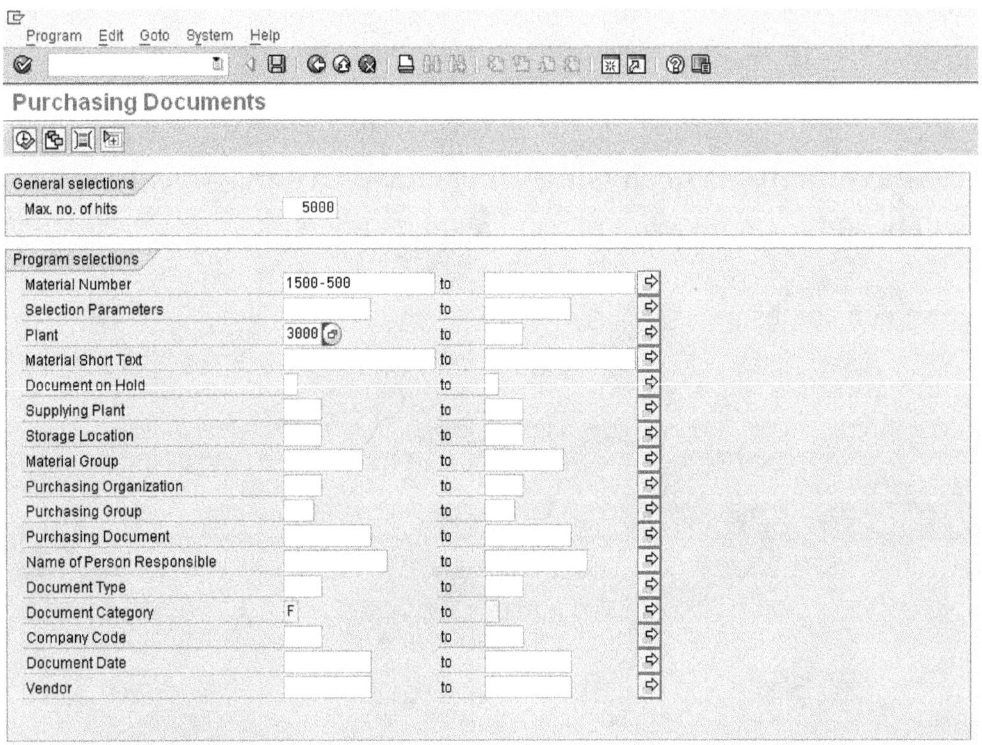

After entering criteria, execute the selection screen to create a list of PO's according to the criteria.

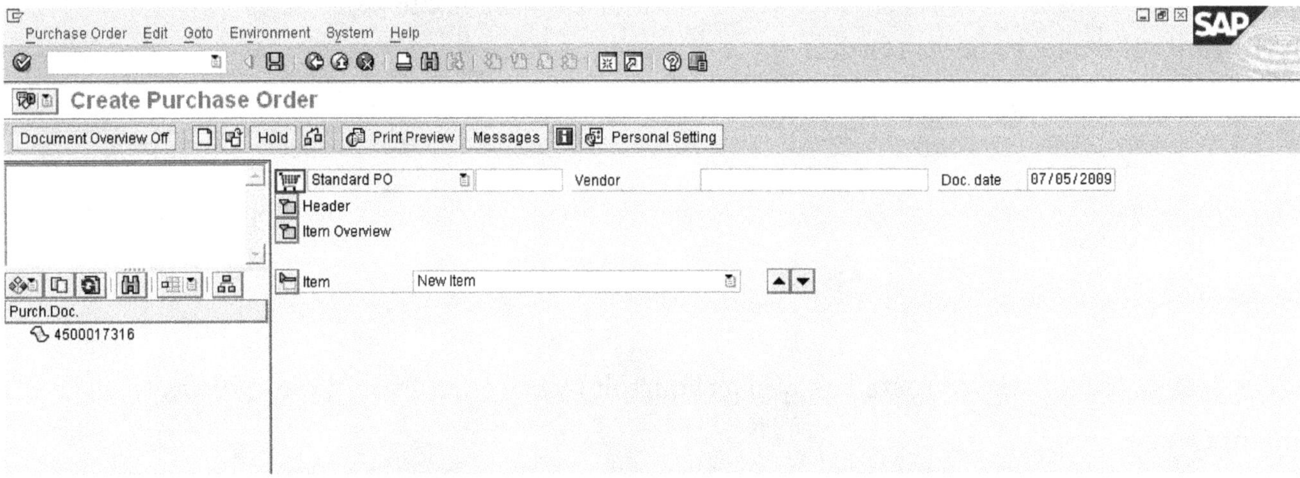

A list in the Document Overview shows PO's fulfilling the criteria selected. In this example, there is only one PO, the PO we created earlier.

Highlight Purchase Order Document that you're interested in, in this case, ▷ 4500017316 and then select **ADOPT** to populate the PO screen with information from the **highlighted** PO.

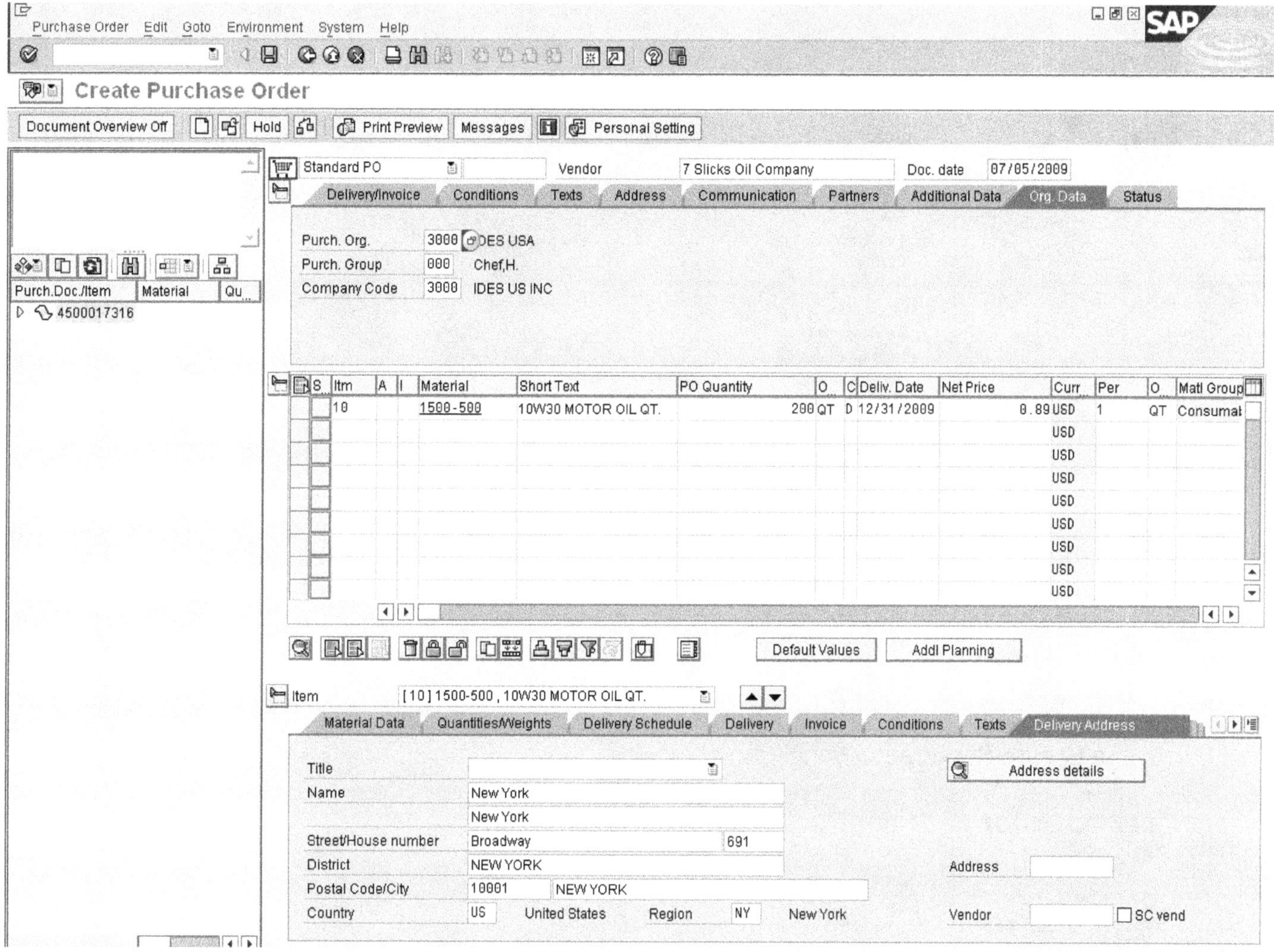

You can now change the quantities, delivery dates and so on and create a new Purchase Order. Select Save when complete.

Purchase Order Document Overview

You can also change the layout of the Document Overview to make it easier to determine which PO you want to select when lists are large. Under the Document Overview section click on the **Change Breakdown** icon. When you do this, the **Change Layout** pop-up window appears.

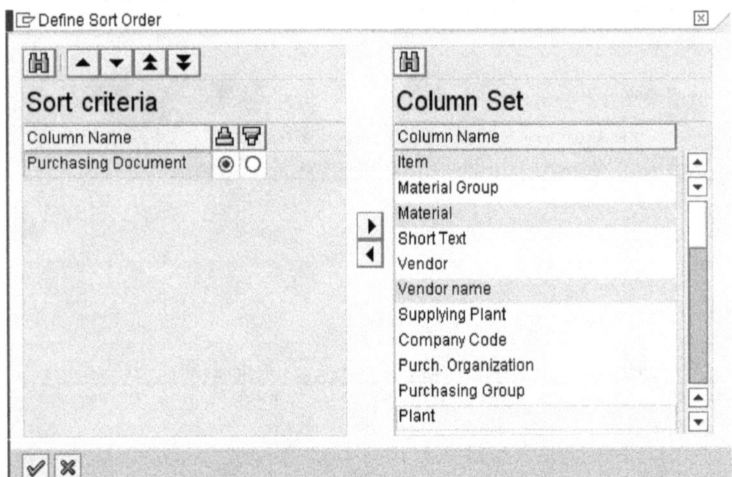

Here you can add sort criteria on the PO list to show up. Select the details from the Column Set you want to see and add them over and then enter. In this case we want **Item, Material, Vendor Name** and **Plant** added. Highlight the fields and click on the black left arrow and then select the green check mark. You can now drill down on the PO to help determine which PO you want to ADOPT to the Create PO screen.

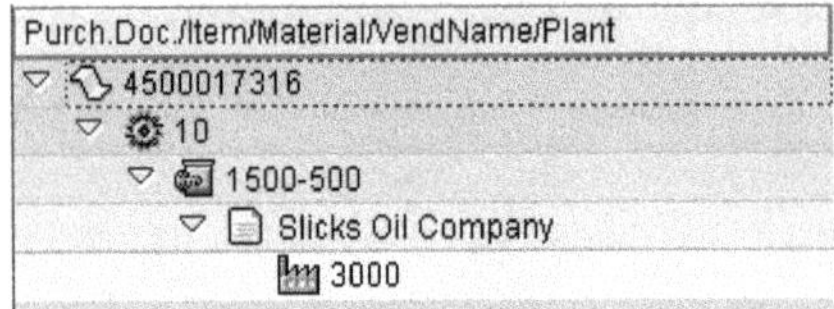

If you like a particular Overview Layout, select the **Save Layout** icon, enter a Layout name and description. Select the User-specific box if you like and then SAVE.

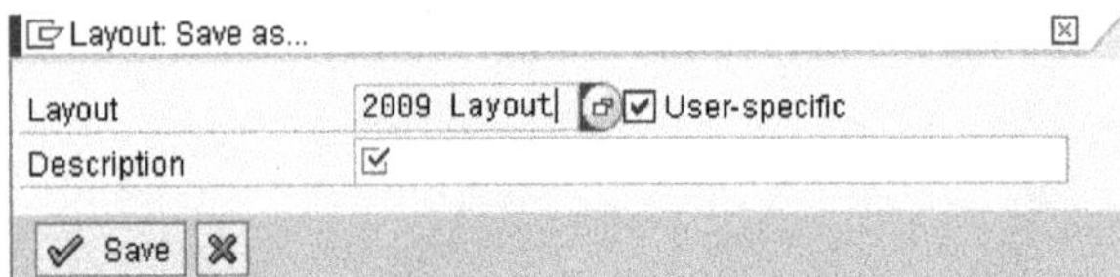

And now when entering the Document Overview, select the choose layout button, select your layout and the layout will display according to your settings.

ME2M Create a Purchase Order List Report

Objective: To create a report of purchase orders created. A report is also referred to as a List Display in SAP

SAP Menu Path:

> **Logistics > Materials Management > Purchasing > Purchase Order > List Display > ME2M-By Material**

(Other "By Lists" could be selected)

Purchasing Documents for Material screen comes up:

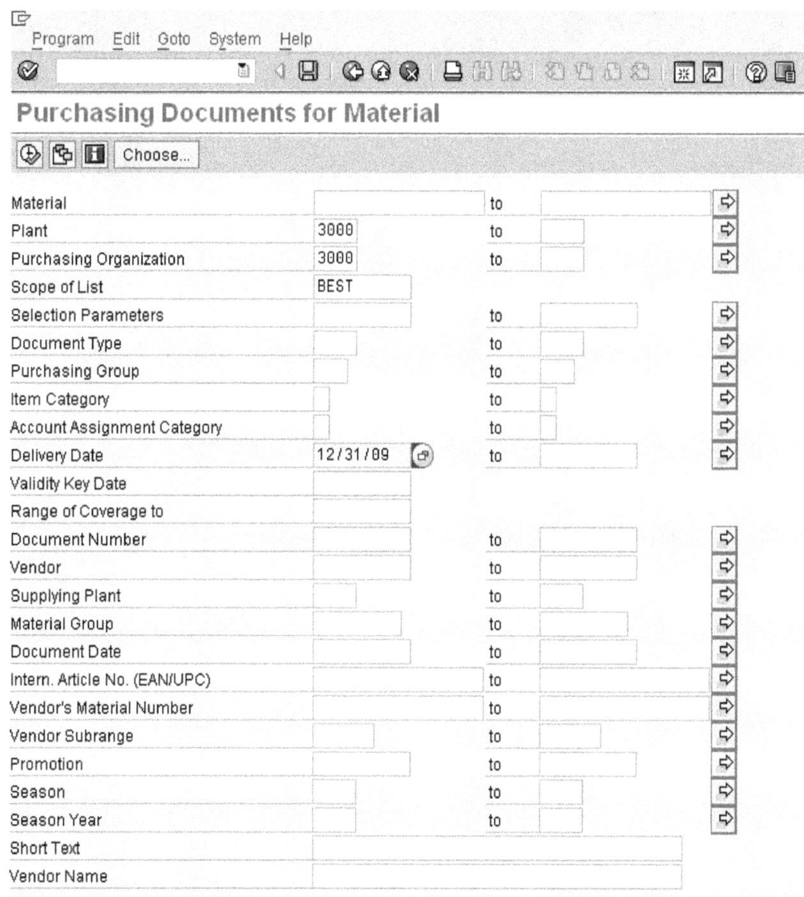

We can select a number of criteria on the first page such as Plant, Purchasing Organization and Delivery Date and so on. When ready, select Execute.

ME2M Create a Purchase Order List Report

The Purchasing Documents for Materials list comes up for the material and criteria requested.

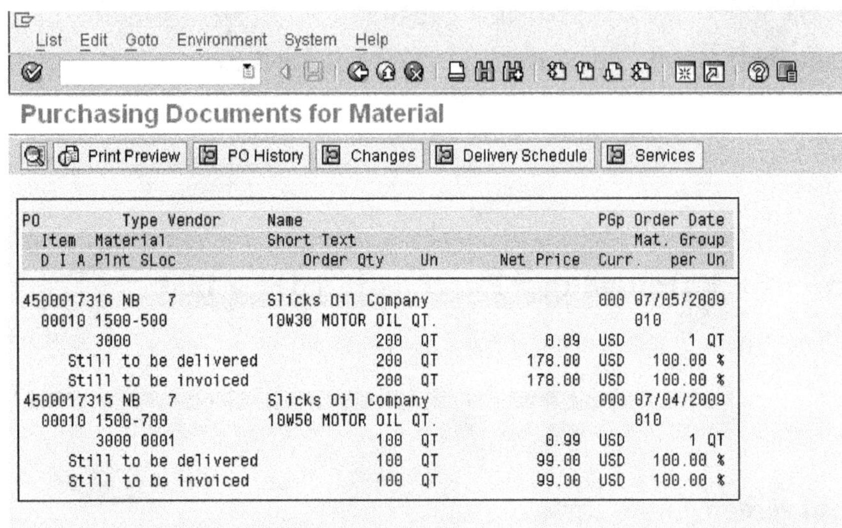

MMRV Check Posting Period for a Company Code

Objective: To CHECK what the current posting period is for a company code prior to posting a goods receipt.

Prior to posting a goods receipt, a posting period for a given company code must be open. A posting period needs to be opened at the beginning of a given period, usually the first of the month. To check what the current posting period is for a company code, follow:

SAP Menu Path:

> **Logistics > Production – Process > Process Order > Environment > Master Data > Material Master > Other > MMRV –Allow Posting Period to Previous Period**

The **Allow Posting Period to Previous Period** screen comes up. Here we enter the Company Code we are interested in posting our Goods Receipt to, in this case Company Code 3000.

Select the green check or Enter, and the Posting Periods for the company code comes up.

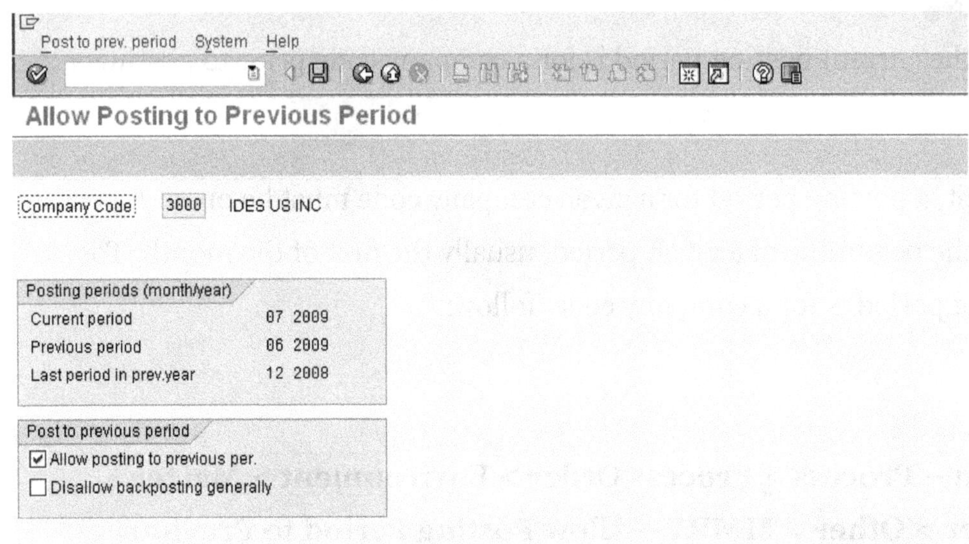

Here we see that for Company Code 3000 we are currently posting in the month of July of 2009. We are also able to back post in the previous period of June 2009. So if this were the month of August of 2009, we could not post to company code 3000 until we opened up August 2009 using transaction code MMPV.

MMPV Change Posting Period for a Company Code

Objective: To CHANGE what the current posting period is for a company code prior to posting a goods receipt.

NOTE: ONLY DO THIS ON THE FIRST OF THE MONTH AND ONLY IF YOU ATTEMPTED TO POST A GOODS RECEIPT AND CHECKED THAT THE POSTING PERIOD NEEDS TO BE CHANGED.

To change the current posting period for a company code, you need to close the last period and open up the new period. GOODS RECEIPT

SAP Menu Path:

> **Logistics > Production – Process > Process Order > Environment > Master Data > Material Master > Other > MMPV- Close Period**

The **Close Period for Material Master Records** screen comes up. Here we enter the company code, new period, Fiscal Year and select the check and close radio button where SAP will check before closing the period and opening a new on. When ready, select Execute.

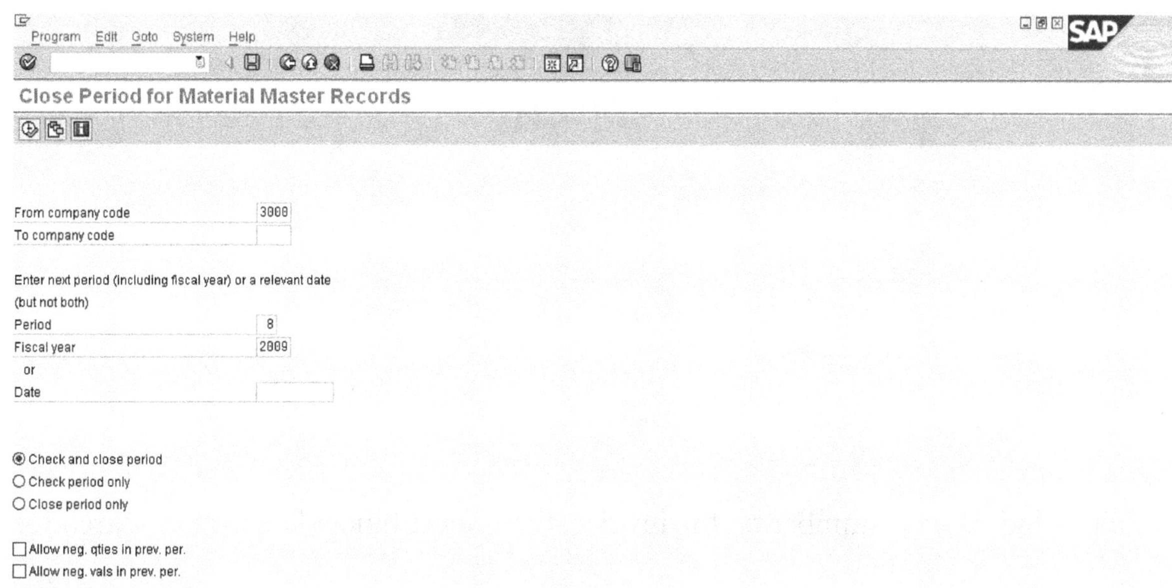

If it passes the check, SAP will complete the period conversion and allow postings in the new period. You can now post a goods receipt to the company code.

MIGO Goods Receipt of Purchase Order

Objective: To make a goods receipt to a companies stock while referencing a specific purchase order.

We have created a purchase requisition and in turn created a purchase order from that requisition. After submitting the order to the vendor, the vendor has shipped the product to us and we need to receive it into SAP. We do this using transaction code MIGO.

SAP Menu Path:

> **Logistics > Materials Management > Purchasing > Purchase Order > Follow-On Functions > MIGO - Goods Receipt**

The Goods Receipt Purchase Order screen comes up.

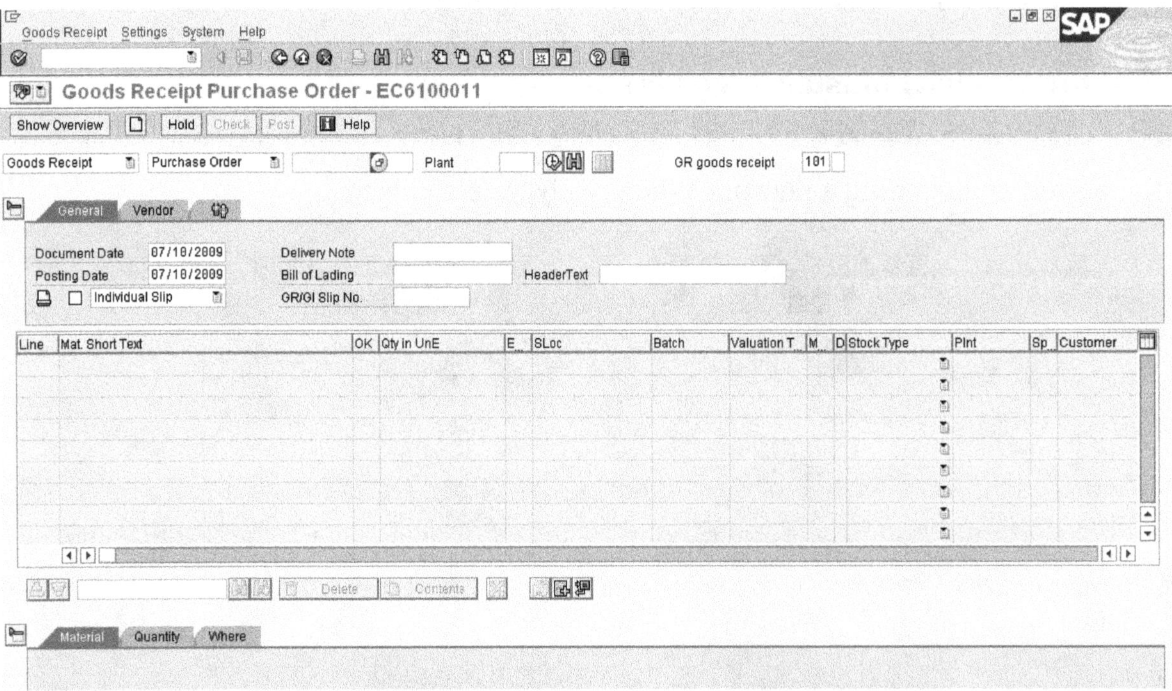

If the supplier didn't include the PO number on the invoice, then select binoculars icon to search for it.

The Goods Receipt Purchase Order pop-up window appears. Here we enter a vendor and delivery date then select FIND. We could also enter other data to help us find the correct Purchase Order number associated with the goods receipt.

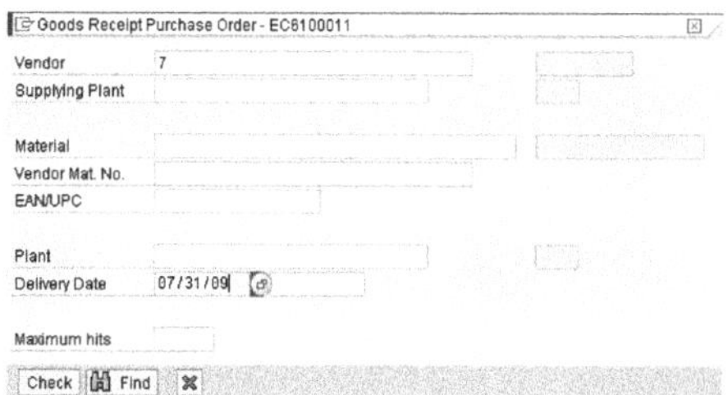

A list of Purchase Orders comes up at the bottom of the screen.

Select the order number, under the Purchase Document header, and then select ADOPT icon. This populates the **Goods Receipt Purchase Order** screen. Close the Purchase Order search results window by selecting **X** icon.

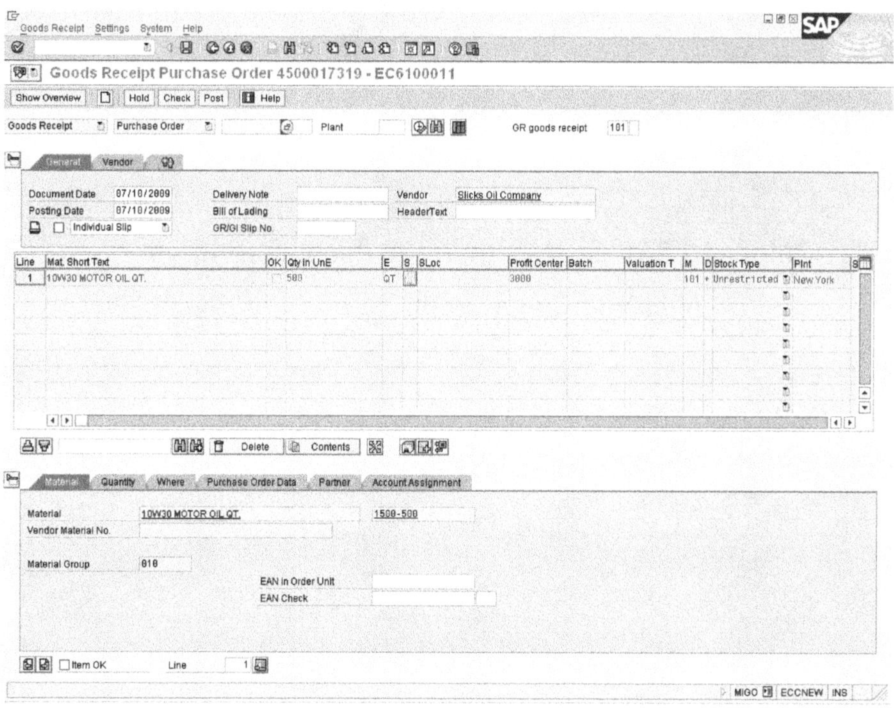

MIGO Goods Receipt of Purchase Order

At the bottom of Goods Receipt screen, check the Item OK box, assuming you checked over the goods and they appear undamaged.

On the Item Details under the "Where" tab, enter a storage location.

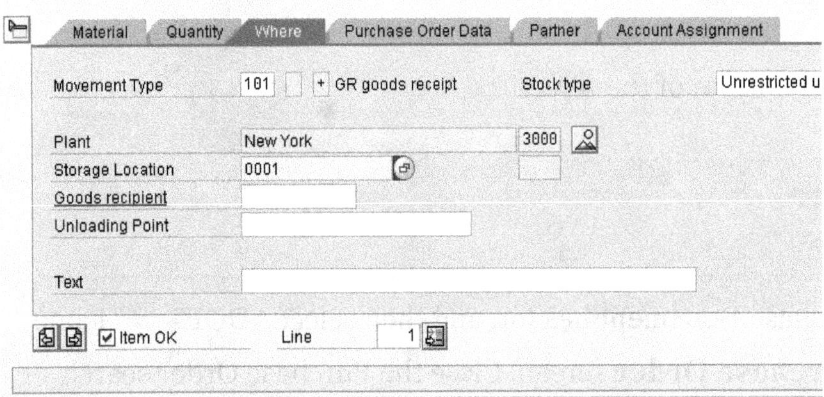

Next click on the CHECK button Hold Check Post at the top of the screen and then SAP verifies if the document is OK.

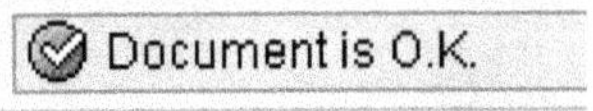

Select the SAVE icon to save the goods receipt and SAP issues a material document number.

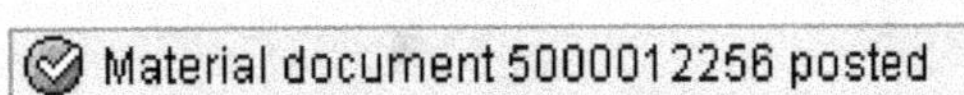

Index

www.ingramcontent.com/pod-product-compliance
Lightning Source LLC
Chambersburg PA
CBHW060204060326
40690CB00018B/4237
9781603321303